MW00827041

FROM THE DUNGEONS OF NORTH VIETNAM

Return With Honor
March 4, 1973

by

Lt. Col. A.T. Ballard, Jr. USAF (Ret.)

Carrie's Creek

ISBN: 978-0-578-18795-2

Library of Congress Control Number: 2016961796

PRINTED IN THE UNITED STATES OF AMERICA

INTRODUCTION AND DEDICATION

My purpose in writing of my experiences as a prisoner of war is to add to our family history. The following pages represent the highlights of the first four of my seven years of internment in the dungeons of North Vietnam.

This manuscript is dedicated to my wife, Ruth, who bore those seven difficult years with strength and dignity, while taking her place in the community. I am so proud of her and her accomplishments, and especially of the way she raised our son, Kevin. I never would have written this memoir had it not been for her encouragement, editing, and typing.

Arthur T. Ballard, Jr.
Lt. Col. USAF (Ret.)

LETTER TO MY WIFE

10 Sep 66

Dear Ruth,

It's almost midnight. I've been sitting out on the porch drinking scotch with Thomas and Turley all night, so if you can't read this, neither can I! They had a rough one today. Mike, Turk, and Bob Hannah — all three had their aircrafts shot up pretty bad. They all got back, though, luckily. I wasn't with them because I had to check out my new room mate on a fairly easy target today. His name is Don Quigley — an old ADC pilot. We got 2 of them in yesterday. I worry more about the guys in my flight than I do myself! I think I'll put Mike + Turk in for a silver star medal for that mission today. They did good work.

I feel better tonight. I've had the worries all day. Every time I have this something happens. I guess I just get the jitters every once in a while, having been shot at so many times.

TABLE OF CONTENTS

PART
ONE

POW★MIA

YOU ARE NOT FORGOTTEN

IN THE DUNGEONS

SHOT DOWN AND CAPTURED

September 26, 1966

I was flying the number three position in a flight of four F-lo5's from Korat Air Force Base, Thailand. The weather was clear as we flew across the Red River Valley and toward the target, which was a large oil storage area. Two minutes before we reached the target my aircraft was hit somewhere in the aft section, probably the engine. I called the flight and told them I had been hit. My wingman said, "Roger, three, you are hit."

The cockpit began filling with smoke. I attempted to stop it with the air-conditioning control lever, but it had been knocked loose and was useless. The smoke obscured forward visibility, but I discovered I could see through the top of the canopy. I attempted to maneuver the aircraft to get closer to the target to drop my ordnance before ejecting. Shortly after moving the controls, I became unconscious. Upon regaining consciousness, I again tried to maneuver the aircraft to see the target and again lost consciousness. This happened three or four times. Probably smoke inhalation caused the unconsciousness, because I do not recall any associated pain. During one of the intervals I heard my wingman say, "Bail out, Ted."

When I next became aware of my surroundings, I was on the ground. I have no recollection of the ejection sequence or parachute descent. Perhaps I subconsciously followed the instructions of my wingman.

As I opened my eyes, I noticed that blood was dripping from my head onto my wrist. The time was 0735—approximately twelve minutes from the time my aircraft was hit until I awoke on the ground. My first conscious thoughts were of my wife. I said, "Ruth, I'm sorry. It's going to be a long time."

Taking stock of myself, I realized that my left leg was broken and the right leg was badly sprained. I was lying at the foot of a tree, among what looked like ancient, gnarled roots. My parachute was draped over the tree and, strangely, appeared to be black and white rather than the standard colors of orange and white. I attempted to remove my radio from my vest and call the other members of the flight to let them know that I was alive. I was unsuccessful. Perhaps shock had taken effect and I was in and out of consciousness for the next hour or so.

The next few scenes are fragments of memory… Someone has his arms around me and is lifting my pistol from its holster… The barrel of a rifle is stuck in my face… I am wrapped in my parachute and tied to a long bamboo pole… Many soldiers are making a lot of noise carrying me out of the wooded area…

I became fully awake and realized that I had been stripped of all my clothing except for my underwear. The North Vietnamese soldiers tried to get me to stand up. When I convinced them I could not, two of them, one under each arm, dragged me approximately 200 yards and laid me down in a small clearing near a village.

Thus began six and one-half years of pain, hunger, thirst, fear, anxiety, humiliation, and degradation. There was also hope. And faith.

★ ★ **4** ★ ★

TRAINING CAMP

As I lay there in the grass, several hundred villagers gathered in a circle around me, but kept away and did not harm me. They appeared to be merely curious. Two soldiers kept guard. I asked for water and medical attention for my legs. The answer was "No" for medical attention. Not even a splint. About an hour later, I received a small cup of hot water, along with a cup of rice and sugar mixture. I eventually got the hot water down. I later learned that all drinking water had to be boiled. I was also given bananas.

I was left there in the clearing all day until just after sunset. At this time, a motorcycle arrived that had a sidecar attached. I was put in the sidecar, blindfolded, and tied. Just before we left, someone dropped the stalk of bananas that I had not eaten onto my lap.

We rode for about one hour, stopping periodically at checkpoints, where someone would reach in and pinch me gently.

Finally, we stopped at what I later thought to be a military training camp for boys. I was taken into a small room and placed in a chair, facing a table with a gooseneck lamp on it. A few minutes later three men came into the room and sat behind the table.

Two of the men were in civilian clothes; the other wore a North Vietnamese Army uniform with the insignia of the equivalent of our warrant officer. One of the civilians was a young-looking man, spoke fluent English, and was the only one to speak to me.

He asked the standard questions of name, rank, service number, and date of birth.

I answered these questions as required by the Code of Conduct. I then asked for medical treatment and was ignored. The next question was "What type aircraft were you flying?"

I told him that I could not answer any further questions. He said, "Why not?" I answered that under the terms of the Geneva Convention we were not required to go beyond name, rank, service number, and date of birth. He said, "We did not sign those agreements." I knew that they had been a signatory of the Convention, but did not argue the point. I said, "Anyway, I cannot answer any other questions."

The man in uniform made a motion with his hands, and immediately someone grabbed me from behind, tied me to the chair with a rope, and cinched my arms and hands very tightly behind me. A rope was put around my neck. Tight, but I could still breathe. Next, small rubber tubing was put around the muscles of both arms and twisted down tightly. This was painful and I yelled loudly. I was told to answer the questions, but I refused.

I remained this way for a few minutes, and then two soldiers untied me and dragged me outside. I had heard what sounded like a pep rally going on nearby—loud noises, cheering, etc. Outside, I noticed there were several small buildings, similar to the one in which I had been. There were two to three hundred young Vietnamese boys sitting on benches in a field. They appeared to be in their early teens, and were yelling, "RAH, RAH, RAH."

I could not tell the rank of the soldier who was speaking to them, but he was obviously their leader. The two guards dragged me to the area and threw me across one of the benches in front of the speaker's platform. Needless to say, I was quite frightened, with all the noise along with the pain in my legs. I stayed there for what seemed like five or ten minutes. I looked up at the kids on the front benches and, from their bearing, realized they were as scared as I was and would not look at me. They were dressed in yellow jackets with a wide band that draped from the shoulder to the waist.

The two soldiers dragged me back to the room and threw me onto the floor. They picked me up, tied me to the chair, and used the same technique of torture as before. After a few moments, I became concerned about the circulation in my arms and decided to answer some of their questions. I told them the truth about what type aircraft I had been flying and what target I had been assigned to hit. I was positive that they already knew this information. I lied about my home base, saying that I was stationed at Da Nang Air Force Base, South Vietnam. I also lied about my marriage and the names and numbers of my brothers and sisters. I told them I had two brothers named Charles and Frank; a sister, Ruth; and a cousin, Kevin. They seemed to be satisfied with my answers.

I again asked for medical treatment and was refused. Evidently, it was time to go to Hanoi. They untied me, carried me outside, and placed me in the back of a small jeep-type truck with benches along each side. I was blindfolded with my hands loosely tied in front. The officer drove the truck and the English-speaking civilian sat in back with me.

It was a very long and extremely rough ride to Hanoi. We stopped several times at checkpoints. By the time we got to Hanoi my legs were in bad shape. We arrived just after daybreak on Tuesday morning, September 27, 1966.

THE GREEN ROOM

Several soldiers met us as we arrived at Hoalo jail in downtown Hanoi. They carried me to a room just outside the main complex of cells, laid me on the floor, and departed. I was left alone for approximately thirty minutes. The room was set up exactly like the other one I had been in—desk, three chairs behind, gooseneck lamp, and one chair in front. The walls were green with indentations.

The young English-speaking civilian returned, this time with two different men, both dressed in Army clothes with no insignia. Two guards were very gentle in helping me onto the chair.

The interview began with the questions of name, rank, service number, and date of birth, which I answered. The next question was about my aircraft. By this time I had regained my courage and thought that these people might not be as barbaric as the ones out in the field, so I told them that I was not going to answer any further questions, that it was not required under the terms of the Geneva Convention. I asked for medical treatment for my broken leg.

Immediately I was again tied to the chair in the same manner as before. This time the guard tied or looped ropes around both of my ankles and began pulling my legs back and around the chair. This bending and twisting action was extremely painful. When I began screaming, a rag was stuffed into my mouth. The pain was too much for me to take, so I nodded my head and was untied. I answered the same questions that had been asked the night before.

After about an hour the men left the room. A few moments later one of the men returned with another man dressed in civilian clothes who called himself the camp commander. I asked for water and medical attention. He said, "You will not receive food, water, or medical attention until you have completed all camp formalities." He said that I must give some biographical and military information, and then write a letter to the government of the Democratic Republic of Vietnam condemning the United States government and confessing war crimes. He then asked, "What are your new tactics?"

Two or three weeks prior to my shoot-down, my squadron had been employing a different method of delivering bombs to the target. We were attempting to minimize our losses and gain more accuracy in target destruction.

I attempted to evade the questions by saying that we just came in as fast as we could, dropped the bombs, and got out as fast as we could. He pressed for details with such questions as: "How far from the target do you drop the bombs? What climb angle do you use to drop the bombs? What altitude? What airspeed?"

When I continued to give evasive answers, I was again tied to the chair, and the torture resumed. I knew that if I answered the questions it would mean the shoot-down and possible death of many American pilots, some of whom were my best friends. I refused to answer the questions. I lost consciousness from the pain. When I awakened, the interrogation and torture resumed.

PART ONE: IN THE DUNGEONS

During the next three days, I estimate that I went through between ten and fifteen torture sessions, during most of which I passed out from pain or shock, or a combination of both. My left hip was broken during one of the sessions.

At times, when I awakened, I would find myself untied, on the floor, and alone in the room. Soon the same men would return and the interrogation would begin again, with more questions concerning my military and civilian biography. I gave more detail, but I believe I stuck generally to the same lies I had told earlier.

During this period I was given no food, no water, and no medical attention. I continued to refuse to answer questions concerning military tactics.

Sometime during the evening of September 29, I had again become unconscious from the torture. I looked up when I awakened and saw that the camp commander was the only one in the room. He looked at me and said, "Ballard, answer the question." At this time I was in bad shape and felt that I could not take any more torture. I was nervous, scared, confused, and in great pain. I said a silent prayer that went something like this: "God, please give me the courage to say 'no' to this man one more time." I looked up at him and said, "No." We continued staring at each other for a few moments, and then he gathered his papers and left the room. I was never again asked any questions concerning military tactics.

Later that night a guard brought me a small cup of water. I was placed on a stretcher, put into a truck, and taken to a nearby hospital. The guards laid me on a large table under an antique contraption that the doctor said was an x-ray machine.

Several civilians came through the open door to stand around and look at me. One young man had a small child in his arms. The child was holding a toy machine gun and, when his father pointed me out, turned it toward me and began cranking a handle that made a popping noise. That child had the maddest, meanest look on his face that I have ever seen on anyone so small. I smiled at him and winked. This really surprised him. His eyes opened wide and his mouth dropped open. He looked at his father, who quickly took him outside. The other onlookers stood without expression and seemed not to have noticed the incident.

Several x-rays were taken of my left leg and left hip. The doctor indicated to me that they were both broken. Then there appeared to be an argument between the doctor and the camp commander. I was put on a stretcher and taken back to the camp. This time I was placed on a cement bed in a small cell in "Heartbreak Hotel," part of the Hoalo jail complex. There were shackles for legs embedded in the bed.

It was a very miserable night for me. I do not remember much about it except that I could not sleep, sit, lie, or stand. I pleaded for water and medical attention. I cursed the guards when they walked by the room.

Early the next morning I heard a voice asking me my name. How wonderful to hear another American's voice! We exchanged names. He was evidently in the cell next to mine. He calmed me down and told me to try to keep as quiet as possible because it was dangerous for everyone. At this time a guard came by and I heard no more for several hours.

Later that day the POW attempted to contact me by tapping on the wall. I did not know the tap code, but I thought of using one tap for "A," two taps for "B," three for "C," etc. After establishing communication I told him what they were doing to me. He advised me to write a confession and they would take me to the hospital. We were again interrupted by the guard and I had no more contact with him. I had already made up my mind that I would have to write something, because I could not stand any more torture.

That night I was taken back to the "Green Room." The stretcher was left in the room for me to lie on. The camp commander came in, asked a couple of questions, gave me some papers to read, and departed. There were three separate statements signed by American POWs, two of whom I knew. I glanced through them but could not concentrate. It was another miserable night for me.

The next day was marked with more interrogations concerning my biography; mostly a rehash of previous questions and briefings explaining to me why I was a criminal and the United States was wrong in becoming involved in South Vietnam. I was again told that I would receive no medical attention until I had confessed my crimes and condemned the United States government.

Sometime during the day I was given some rice and a bowl of green soup. I could not eat but managed to drink the broth.

That evening I decided to write, thinking that if I wrote just anything, they would at least leave me alone. I do not recall the exact wording of my first letter (I had to address it to the people and government of the Democratic Republic of Vietnam). In general, I agreed with the policies of our government. The camp commander read it, tore it into small pieces, and said I was wasting his time. I thought I would give it one more try and write a statement similar to one that I had read earlier which really didn't say much of anything. I wrote the following:

"I can understand why the Vietnamese people believe the United States is wrong in being in South Vietnam. Since I am a devout Christian, each night I pray that God will forgive me of all my sins."

I could hardly grip the pen, and my handwriting looked like a childish scrawl. He read it and made me scratch out the phrase "Since I am a devout Christian." I signed it and he said, "Now I take you to hospital."

At the hospital more x-rays were taken, and then I was laid on a platform that was about four feet high with a vertical rod between my legs. A screw-on device was strapped to my feet and was used to straighten my legs. The right leg did not straighten, but remained slightly bent at the knee. My left leg, buttocks, and upper torso were put in a cast. I was left in this position for about thirty minutes to dry.

I was then taken by truck to a camp on the outskirts of Hanoi that was later referred to as the "Zoo." We arrived there about 0100, 2 October 1966.

PIGSTY, ROOM SIX

I was placed on one of two wooden beds in a small twelve-by-twelve cell. When the guards departed I realized I was shaking the hand of Ensign George McSwain, US Navy. George had been living in solitary confinement for about two months and was as glad to see another American as I. George took care of me for a long time under most difficult conditions. I owe a great debt to him.

I do not recall very much of the next few weeks. I was extremely weak and in much pain. My mind was fuzzy and I had to ask George to repeat things that he told me. He tried to make me as comfortable as possible, getting up at frequent intervals throughout the night to attend to my needs. The guards had given me a bedpan and I used this to prop up my left leg because it was too painful to lie flat.

We were issued two sets of pajama-like clothing and two sets of underwear. We also had a pair of tire sandals, toothbrush, toothpaste, mosquito net, tin cup, soap, washcloth, pitcher for water, and a straw mat. There was also a waste bucket. We shaved once a week, which was quite an experience with the dull blades! I found out later that I was number eight to use the blade. The guards gave us a haircut every forty-five days. For the first few weeks George had to shave me because my hands were still almost useless. I seem to remember that he also had to feed me for a while, although George denies this. I could drink the broth from the soup and could eat a little rice. George kept encouraging me to eat more and I eventually could.

George gave me a briefing on the layout of the camp. There were nine buildings with a total of fifty to sixty POWs, none of whom we could contact until February l967. We learned later that the building we lived in was called the Pigsty. It had eleven rooms, or cells, all about the same size. Directly behind our cell was a shower room, and next to it was a latrine—the bowl was used to dump our waste buckets. The cell next to ours was empty. In each room was a loudspeaker with no volume control, which was hooked up to the camp radio. Twice each day we had to listen to "Hanoi Hannah" over the Voice of Vietnam, a local radio station. There was also much propaganda from the camp officials. Frequently we were told that we were criminals and must obey the camp regulations or be punished.

I soon became used to the daily routine. A gong would awaken us at 0500. George would get up, fold our nets and clothing, and sweep out the room with a small whiskbroom. He would then begin exercising, doing some sit-ups and pushups. The turnkey would come around at 0600 and give us each a cigarette and light (we were not allowed to keep matches). At 0700 a guard, usually female, would bring some water for our jugs. Then the turnkey began letting each room out to bathe for about fifteen minutes. When it was our turn, George would bathe himself, empty the waste bucket, wash our dirty clothes, return with a bucket of water, and bathe me.

Around 1100 the chow girls would bring soup and rice and dish it up for us on the porch. George would then be let out by the guard to get our food and bring it back to the room. When we were finished the guard picked up the dishes and placed them outside. Soon two POWs would collect all the dishes and wash them in the shower room. Then another cigarette, another light.

From 1200 to 1400 was "quiet hour." During this time we were required to lie on our beds. It was quiet in the camp, with only the guards periodically checking on us by silently opening the hatch in the door to peer in.

The gong would clang again at 1400 and the camp would come alive. Those rooms that had not bathed in the morning would do so. Water and chow again at about 1700, followed by the last cigarette of the day. George smoked very little, so I usually had the luxury of an extra cigarette each time.

At 2100, the gong would sound, signifying bedtime. George would put up our mosquito nets and then he would lie down and try to sleep. Because of the pain and being so uncomfortable I could sleep for only ten to twenty minutes at a time for a total of about two hours per night.

Periodically, throughout the day, the routine was broken by the guards harassing the prisoners. We could hear them yelling at the POWs and beating them up. Every time a Vietnamese came into our room, or just looked in, George stood up and bowed. I asked George why he did this and he said, "They tied me up and beat the shit out of me until I agreed to bow." I was to learn later just what he meant. All the POWs were forced to bow.

Once each week an inspection of the room was held. A Vietnamese officer and several guards would come into the room and check every article of clothing, the beds, and windows. George would have to stand facing the wall and be searched.

At night, while lying awake, I would observe lizards that inhabited our room. They were geckoes and could change their shades of color. Over the years I became very fond of these creatures and could write a small book about them.

Our cell was dimly lit with a twenty-five-watt bulb. The cord came in through a vent near the ceiling, and the bulb lay against the wall. The lizards spent most of their time there to catch insects and to keep warm in the winter.

It was quiet in the camp at night. I could hear the guards making their rounds, checking the cells. One guard's favorite position was just outside our window. Sometimes I could hear his snoring. Several dogs were in the camp. They were not watchdogs but were raised and were fattened to be eaten by the Vietnamese. As far as I know we were never fed dog meat. It was evidently a delicacy reserved for the Vietnamese.

Sometimes the quiet of the night would be disturbed by a long convoy of trucks that passed nearby, heading south. An occasional air raid would liven things up. I had a feeling of helplessness when the bombs were dropping nearby, but I comforted myself with the belief that the pilots knew the location of the POW camps.

Mostly my thoughts centered around my wife, Ruth, and our son, Kevin, wondering how they were and how the news of my shoot-down had affected them. I knew that my wife was a strong person and that I would be very proud of her.

During the day, George and I exchanged biographies and talked of many things. I grew to love George and thought of him as a brother. I have often considered writing a book and entitling it *Ensign George McSwain*. Briefly, he is about six feet tall with black hair and brown eyes, a bachelor from Montrose, California, just turned twenty-five years old. George spent two years with the Army paratroopers, two years in college, and was shot down by a SAM missile just a few months after being commissioned.

We felt that it was going to be a long war and talked about how to conduct ourselves. We agreed to follow the Code of Conduct as best we could and to give the enemy as little as possible. If we were temporarily broken by torture, as soon as we recovered we would begin resisting again.

About once a week George was taken to one of several rooms in an administration building. There he would be interrogated by a Vietnamese officer. These quizzes usually lasted for one hour. Very little new information was sought. It was a short rehash of biographical information followed by a recitation of propaganda decrying the presence of the United States in South Vietnam.

One day in early November 1966, an officer, whom we called "J.C.," sat down next to my bed, holding a pen and paper, evidently ready to take dictation. Of the Vietnamese interrogators, J.C. was known to be one of the meanest and most ruthless. He never came around the POWs without an armed guard.

J.C. began by asking some simple biographical questions, which I answered. Then he told me that the United States was the criminal in South Vietnam and should get out. He said, "What are your feelings about that?" I said, "The United States is right being in South Vietnam and will stay there to prevent the North Vietnamese from taking over the South."

J.C. curled his lips and said, "The camp commander at the other camp told me about you. You are a die-hard. You have not confessed your crimes!" I said, "No, and I am not going to. I am not a criminal." He jumped up and shouted, "Your future is very dark! Soon you will be punished!" He stormed out of the cell, shouting to the guards.

After the door was locked, George said that I had probably made a mistake, that the Vietnamese were stupid, that one could usually talk around some topics and not really say anything.

The next day, while George was outside bathing, I noticed an armed guard looking through the door at me. He had a rifle slung across his shoulder and his right hand was fondling a knife that was in its sheath. He looked around the courtyard and then slowly walked into the room. He came to my bed and suddenly drew the knife and came down toward my face with it. Just as the tip of the blade touched my face, it was as if an invisible shield stopped the thrust. Immediately the guard returned the knife to the sheath and left the room. I never blinked an eye during the entire ordeal.

A few days later, on November 5, 1966, a loose nail was found in a crack in the wall, near a window in our cell. George was accused of "plotting the blackest of crimes against the Vietnamese people," and for punishment had to stand facing the wall with his arms straight up over his head. This form of torture was for fourteen hours each day, seven days a week. It lasted for seven weeks. He was allowed no bath nor shave. For variation they made him stand in the same position in the middle of the room. He was frequently beaten and slapped by the guards.

After about a week of this, George was taken to quiz and returned with pen and paper. J.C. had told him that if I would confess to being a war criminal and condemn the United States government,

George would be taken off punishment. George looked at me and said, "Don't do anything on my account. I can take it."

I thought about it for a while and decided to write the same statement that they had tortured me for in the "Green Room." I figured it would not satisfy J.C. but it was worth a try. George took the paper with him to the next quiz. When the guard brought him back and put him "on the wall," George said, "He didn't buy it."

I said, "I'm sorry, George."

George said, "I know. Don't sweat it."

Lying on my bed in my cast, I was facing the door. This was a big advantage for us because I could clear for George to allow him to rest his arms. This was infrequent, though, because the guards seemed to hang around most of the day to harass him.

To keep our minds occupied and to encourage George, we would tell each other of our experiences. And we played word games. I can still picture George "holding up the wall" and naming all the girls he could think of that started with the letter A, then B, etc. Then I would name those I could think of. One day it was my turn and we were working on the R's. I was tired, sleepy, and extremely uncomfortable in my cast. I named a few but then couldn't think of any more. George said, "There's one more." I thought for a few minutes and said, "I've exhausted my supply. What is it?" He said, "Ruth, you blockhead!"

The weather turned cold in November. George had tied my shorts around my feet to keep them warm, but J.C. made him take them off, saying that we were committing crimes against the "People's Clothing." In late November we were given two blankets.

On November 26, 1966, a guard came in, pulled out a pocketknife, and cut off my cast. He handed me a pair of crutches and said, "Walk." I was so weak I could not sit up nor move my left leg. When George thought the guards were not nearby he would come "off the wall" and gently exercise my leg, massaging it and moving it very carefully. Sometimes the guard would catch him, come in, and slap him around.

It took several days for me to get enough strength to sit up and then use the crutches. Slowly I began to walk around the room. I cannot describe my happy feeling to be free of that bed and to be able to hobble around the room on those crutches. I thought to myself, *Someday I'll walk without the crutches. Maybe I can use them as weapons to escape.*

George said he would give me a bottle of booze if I could walk without the crutches by the end of the year. I said, "Okay, I'll accept that bet." He said, "It's not a bet. I'll give you a bottle."

December 24th came and George was still "holding up the wall." As evening approached, a guard came and took George to quiz. While he was gone I suddenly felt inspired to walk without the crutches. I carried them with me, but did not use them. I made it all the way around the room. I had given myself a Christmas present and waited impatiently for George to come back so I could tell him.

When George returned he had a few pieces of sugar candy and an extra cigarette for each of us. This was a pleasant surprise since I never thought the Vietnamese would recognize Christmas. George said the quiz room was full of oranges and bananas and we would receive some later. We never did.

Later some Christmas music was played over the camp radio. A POW sang two or three songs. I wondered who he was but never found out.

It was a sad Christmas Eve for us. As we went to bed, George was silent and despondent. We did not talk as we normally did. I could imagine his thoughts. Mine were of my family and Christmases past.

The gong did not clang as usual Christmas morning. However, a guard came by and told George to "get on the wall." About three hours later he was taken to quiz and J.C. told him that the camp commander had forgiven him of his "crimes" and that George must obey the camp regulations. We were both jubilant at this news. George's long ordeal was over. In a way we felt it was a victory for us since I did not have to write a confession or condemn the United States. Several times I came close to calling a halt to the torture and writing the statement, but George was a tough man and he took it as he said he could.

It was quite a sight watching George shave that long beard off!

The Vietnamese gave us a good Christmas dinner—a piece of meat, lots of rice, and for the first time, cabbage soup.

In January I ventured outside for the first time with George during our daily ten- to fifteen-minute bathing period. Sometimes we used a slow-running faucet in the shower room. No hot water. There was also a well near our building that we used periodically. It surely felt great to get outside, however briefly. George had described the layout of the camp to me, but I was surprised to see how close the buildings were to each other. They looked similar to ours with the same number of cells. Each cell, except for the building called the "Pool Hall," had a window with louvered shutters.

The guards began harassing me about bowing. I got by with only a slight lean forward, complaining that it hurt my hip to bend over, which it did.

In January I had my first quiz in the administration building. I was still using one crutch when I went outside and I went barefoot because it was difficult to walk in those tire sandals. The officer sitting behind the desk, later known as the "Rat," was a small skinny man, about five feet tall. I nodded to him, leaned my crutch against the desk, and sat down on a small stool in front of the desk. The quiz started with a few biographical questions, followed by forty-five minutes of propaganda. I did not argue any of his points. In fact, I said nothing at all. When he finished he said, "Now, go back to your room."

Later, when communications were established between rooms and buildings, we referred to this type of interrogation as "BS." Example: "Today Joe had BS quiz with Pig." If the quiz varied significantly we would give details.

George and I both lost a great deal of weight during those first few months. I was in good physical condition when I was shot down, 180 pounds, waist thirty-three inches. In February 1967, I estimated my weight to be 125 to 130 pounds, and my waist about twenty-four inches.

In late January and early February, more POWs moved into the Zoo from other camps. The total in the camp was about 120. Three men moved in next to us, so George and I finally could communicate with other Americans. This was a big morale boost for us. There were thirty POWs in our building, the Pigsty.

It was announced over the radio that all POWs were to receive injections for cholera and some other diseases. George and I never received any.

Communicating with other POWs was strictly forbidden and many men were tortured because of it. In our cell, George would hang onto the bars in the window and watch for the guards while I tapped on the wall to our neighbors. This was standard clearing procedure throughout the camp. Some men could not see out of their room and would have to rely on hearing the guards approach or seeing the shadow move under the door. We communicated between rooms by using a tap code, and between buildings by using a hand code.

Harassment by the guards was a continuing thing, along with beatings and other forms of torture. Many men were in leg irons for various reasons.

TET, the Vietnamese Lunar New Year, came in February and we were again given a good meal. Everyone was given about two ounces of wine that the guards said was made from oranges. I began to wish for more Vietnamese holidays!

Another important event occurred in February. I quit using my crutches entirely! Even though my leg and hip continued to ache, I felt I could improve by exercising and walking without them.

One morning in early May, I was looking outside through a crack in the door and saw my old friend Burt coming to empty his "bo" (Vietnamese for waste bucket). Burt was the first pilot in my squadron to be shot down. I wanted to whisper to him as he passed our window and give him news about his family. I told George to climb onto the other window and clear for me. Just as George looked out the window, a guard came around the corner and saw him. They were face-to-face. Ten minutes later George was in leg irons and tight wrist cuffs, with his arms behind him. The leg irons were tied to the bed. George was in a most painful position and stayed that way for two days and nights. The cuffs cut into his wrists. I attempted to make him as comfortable as possible by propping him up with blankets, but the guards would have none of this.

The cuffs were taken off long enough for him to eat but were back on again as soon as he finished. George was not given any cigarettes, but when the two POWs came by to pick up the dirty dishes, they would throw their cigarettes into our room provided the guards were not looking. Words of encouragement came from the other POWs in the Pigsty. There was always a warm feeling of brotherhood, knowing that when one POW was in trouble, all the others were concerned and praying for him. The simple messages "Keep your chin up" or "Our prayers are with you" meant so much.

On the morning of the third day George was taken out of irons and was told to write a letter of apology to the camp commander. George wrote, "I apologize for climbing onto the window to clean off the spider webs."

Toward the end of May, immediately after a particularly close-by air raid, the Rat opened our hatch and yelled at me, "You have not yet confessed your crimes!" I said, "No." He said, "You will be punished!" and slammed the hatch closed. The Rat was obviously frightened by the bombing and was very nervous and excited.

An hour later he returned and said to me, "Write your feelings about the war, and explain why you are a criminal." He handed me a pen and paper and departed.

George said, "You might as well write it and save yourself some torture. Everyone else has."

I decided not to mince any words and wrote the following statement: "I have not killed any women or children or bombed any hospitals. I am not a criminal. I am a prisoner of war." George read it and said, "Boy, that ought to bring some action." A guard came by and took the paper.

The next evening I was told to pack up. I was moving out. As George helped me roll up my few belongings, I thanked him for all he had done for me. We shook hands. I did not see him again for more than three years, but I kept track of him. He is a tough man, that George McSwain.

PIGSTY, ROOM ELEVEN

A turnkey we called the "Frog" took me to Room 11 on the backside of the Pigsty. This room was also adjacent to the shower. Shortly, two more men moved in with me. We soon learned that a major room shuffle had taken place throughout the camp.

My two new cellmates were Bob and Tom, an F-105 Wild Weasel crew shot down in August 1966. Their job had been to locate and destroy surface-to-air missile sites. Anti-aircraft fire got them while they were tracking a target.

Bob was a short, well-built man, about my age, married with one son the same age as mine. Tom was a few years younger and had been married for only three months before going to Southeast Asia. They both had been tortured with ropes.

Tom had developed appendicitis shortly after being captured, and the Vietnamese used this as a tool to gain concessions. When they finally agreed to give him medical treatment, Tom walked from his bed to the truck, and was taken to a hospital. He walked from the truck to the operating table, where his appendix was removed. No anesthesia was given. After he was sutured he walked back to the truck, went back to the Zoo, and finally walked to his bed. Tom was still weak but, like me, could do a few exercises in the mornings.

We had no contact with a few of the buildings in the camp, but we had an accurate count of the number of POWs. Attempting to acquire the names of every American was top priority for me. I knew this would be important information to have in case of an escape or eventual release. At this point I had about seventy-five names on my list. I used a memory technique I had learned in a book written by Mr. Harry Lorayne. It took me a long time to recall and formulate the different methods of memorization. In later years this was a very useful tool for many POWs.

(I had the privilege of meeting Mr. Lorayne in the fall of 1973 when we both appeared on the *To Tell The Truth* television program in New York. I also was honored by his printing an excerpt from a letter I had written him on the cover of his next book. Further, in a *Reader's Digest* article about Mr. Lorayne, he mentioned that his most prized letter was the one he received from me.)

We felt that it was important to have visual identification also. We spent many hours looking through cracks to catch a glimpse of POWs as they passed by going to bathe.

One day, the guard took the three of us around to the front side of the building to sweep off the porch. Tom told him we did not know how to sweep, so the guard proceeded to demonstrate. Tom asked him to show us again. This happened several times. While this was going on I slowly backed up to the window of Room 6 for identification purposes. One of the men who lived there was Norm McDaniel, a black American from North Carolina. As I reached the wall, I heard this voice from above my head whisper, "Look up to yo right." I looked up over my left shoulder and he said, "Yo other right!" All I could see were the whites of two eyes staring down at me. I told him who we were and what room we lived in. Norm said, "Rogah, Room Leben!"

The summer of 1967 was a bad one for the POWs. Two men were caught communicating and were tortured with ropes. They eventually gave the Vietnamese the tap code we were using, and the long, torturous camp purge began. Daily beatings were frequent throughout the camp. Our captors wanted to stop the communicating and get the POWs to write propaganda statements. Many men were put in solitary confinement, tortured with ropes, or placed in irons.

One morning Bob was told to pack up. He was being moved to another room. That afternoon Tom also moved out. I was left alone to wonder what they were going to do to me. Early the next morning I was taken to quiz with the Rat. He gave me a thirty-minute lecture on why I was a criminal. He then handed me a sheet of paper and a pen and told me to write a letter to the people and government of the Democratic Republic of Vietnam, confessing to be a war criminal and condemning the United States government.

I was nervous and really scared. I thought, "Here we go again." I was still quite weak and knew that I could not take much more torture, if any. It would be so easy to write whatever he wanted. I had been through enough torture. But I decided I would go down fighting. I wrote the following: "I agree with and support the policies of the United States government. I consider myself to be a prisoner of war, not a criminal." I signed it and handed it to the Rat.

I could see the tension build up in the Rat's face as he read the statement. When he finished, he took a swing at my head, but

I ducked. He ranted and raved and threatened me with much torture. He then grabbed the paper and ran out of the room. I thought he had gone to get the "goon-squad," but apparently he went to consult with his superior, because he returned about ten minutes later and appeared to be calmed down somewhat. He said, "I will explain to you again why you are a criminal." Another thirty-minute propaganda lecture. He handed me pen and paper and said, "Now, write your confession or you will be severely punished."

I wrote the same statement again, word for word.

The above scene repeated itself four more times before the day was over. By nightfall the Rat was really chomping at the bit. Finally, sometime in the evening, he handed me pen and paper and said wearily, "Go to your room and think about your crimes. I will come in the morning for the paper. If you have not written your confession, your future is very dark."

The next morning I wrote the same statement for the seventh time. Bob and Tom moved back to my cell and I let them read the statement.

A little later the Rat came by and opened the hatch. I handed him the paper. He read it and then silently closed the hatch. I was never again asked to write a confession or condemn the United States government.

I passed a message to the building senior ranking officer (SRO), Major Alan, and advised him of what had taken place. He had recently been severely beaten and was presently solo in leg irons and tight wrist cuffs. His arms were swollen more than twice their normal size. Yet, he still had the courage to tap out a message with the cuffs, encouraging the rest of us and telling us to resist as long as possible without incurring permanent physical or mental damage. He also initiated a "Home for Christmas" prayer. Each day after the noon meal a signal was passed to all rooms. We would then recite the Lord's Prayer.

Harassment by the guards was continuous. Bob was the senior ranking man in our room and was slapped around by the guards periodically. Several times we had to stand with our arms over our heads for a couple of hours at a time. Sometimes Bob and Tom would have to kneel down. Due to my hip injury I could not kneel, so I had to stand at attention for long periods.

In back of the Pigsty was a small building we called the "Outhouse." This building was used for solitary confinement and torture. Earlier, when I lived with George McSwain, I had discovered that the light to the Outhouse was controlled by a switch located in the shower room of the Pigsty. We used the switch to flash coded messages to the occupant—news of the camp and words of encouragement. J.J. lived there for a while. He had lost the use of his hands from torture and would use his wrists and arms to pick up his soup and rice bowls that the guard had placed on the ground in front of the door. A few times he was allowed to bathe in the shower next to our room. When the guards left him alone he would tap messages to us by using his wrists or elbows.

Food rations were meager that fall. For a short time we were given bread instead of rice. Also a small ration of sugar. We were always the last ones to be let out of our room to pick up our food. I would put some of my sugar or other food into J.J.'s plate. The guard saw me do this one day and was very angry at first, but he never stopped me.

J.J. was a very courageous young man. I wish I could have met him personally, but this was not to be. He died in camp sometime later, probably from injuries received from torture or lack of medical attention.

THE STABLES

The following camp regulations were posted in each cell:

1. All criminals must show polite attitude at all times to the officers and guards in the camp or they will be severely punished.

2. All criminals will bow to all officers, guards, and Vietnamese in the camp.

3. Any criminal who attempts to escape, or help others to do so, will be severely punished.

4. Criminals are forbidden to communicate with each other in any way, such as signals and tapping on the walls.

5. All criminals will truthfully answer orally or in writing any question, or do anything directed by the camp authorities.

6. Criminals who follow these camp regulations and who show a good attitude by concrete acts and report all those who want to make trouble will be rewarded and shown humane treatment.

All the POWs had a rough time during the summer and fall of 1967. The Vietnamese had many different programs going at the same time. Some men were forced to go to downtown Hanoi and be interviewed by foreign delegations. Some went without being tortured. The guards took groups of two or three POWs to dig foxholes in the courtyard. Some men refused and were tortured until they agreed to dig. Others dug without being tortured. Announcements were made over the camp radio that all POWs would be required to work both inside and outside the camp. All POWs would be put on trial as criminals. The Vietnamese never referred to us as prisoners of war—we were criminals, sometimes the "blackest of criminals." We were told that we would be tried as criminals and our statements would be sent to the Bertrand Russell War Crimes Trial as evidence. Some POWs would go home after the war, some would spend various periods in prison after the war, and others would be executed.

Bob, Tom, and I had some fairly heated discussions about what to do if we were asked to do any work. I was in favor of not doing anything for them without being tortured. Bob said we would be tortured and would end up digging the foxholes anyway, and would also have to write propaganda statements.

The days and weeks passed. The guards were taking one room at a time out to work or to be tortured. The hardest part of all was wondering when we would be next. For some unknown reason we had received no guidance or orders from the senior ranking officer.

Finally, the Rat came into our cell and said, "What work will you do for the Vietnamese people?" Bob said, "We are not going to do any work." The Rat and the guards departed without saying anything else.

I was very proud of Bob that day.

There were many signs posted around the camp on which were painted such things as "What have you done for peace?" I assumed that whoever did the signs had been tortured to do them. One day at quiz I was asked what I would do to work for peace and end the war. I said, "Nothing." No more was ever said about it.

Tom was asked, "What have you done to help end the war?" Tom said, "I keep my room clean."

The men next door had seen us once while we were outside and asked who was who. Tom tapped, "The short, well-built one is Bob. The tall, thin one is Ted. The good-looking one is Tom!"

The bombing was heavy that fall. We were told to get under our wooden beds during all air raids. One day the U.S. bombed an ammunition dump nearby. I was under the bed with my bad legs sticking out from underneath. Suddenly I had the feeling I should draw my legs up. As soon as I had them underneath the bed a huge clump of plaster fell from the ceiling and hit right where my legs had been.

Later we found some small pellets from anti-personnel cluster bombs that had ricocheted into our cell. The ammo-dump burned for several days. As far as I know no POW was ever injured from the bombings.

Food was rather meager during this period. For several weeks we had nothing but a small bowl of rice and some fish scales and bones twice each day.

Harassment by the guards was continuous. The camp SRO and his cellmates were isolated and tortured with wrist-irons and leg-irons for thirty days, then tortured with "ropes." Ultimately the camp SRO was kept in irons more than eight months.

Sometime during that summer we received messages that two Spanish-speaking Caucasians (we assumed they were Cubans) were in the camp and had selected about twelve POWs to exploit. The POWs were housed in a building we called the Stables. The apparent leader of the two-man team was a big man, six feet one inch tall, and burly. We called him "Fidel." Evidently he was influential with the Vietnamese because he had been given free reign with that group of POWs. The other man was smaller, about five feet eight inches, with salt-and-pepper hair. We called him "Chico." Fidel spoke English very well and had a good understanding of American slang. He also had a very bad and quick temper. Chico seemed to be more even-tempered and played the role of the "nice guy" most of the time.

Various cells in the camp were used as torture cells to get each POW to "submit" to Fidel. The first two men were "submitted" within a few days by the use of extreme torture. This quick and sure method was taught to Fidel by the Vietnamese. Fidel experimented with more sophisticated methods with the other men and took notes of their reactions. He wanted to gain submission without using torture but was unsuccessful.

The methodical submitting of the remaining ten POWs took about four months. Fidel wanted a complete surrender to the point where the POW would do anything Fidel told him to do, including making tape recordings and writing propaganda material and "Call L.B.J. a son of a bitch."

All during the four months, the entire group was interrogated daily on an individual basis. The tactics employed ran the gauntlet from Chico's nice-guy approach to Fidel's tirades. They were keeping the men off balance and under constant stress. Fidel would proclaim that the POW must submit totally. There was no middle ground. The POW must see the justness of the struggle of the Vietnamese people. If he supported the U.S. government, then he was a murderer of women and children. If he did not believe in the murder of women and children, then he supported the just struggle of the Vietnamese people. When the POW remained silent or supported his government, Fidel would go into a tirade and proclaim that tomorrow he would turn the POW into a "pile of sheet." The POW was then taken back to his cell and left to worry about the next day's events.

The next day Fidel would tell him that it was time for him to submit and condemn the U.S. government. Then Fidel would turn on a tape recording of classical music and say, "Ah, perhaps tomorrow you will surrender, but today you will enjoy the music, eh?" and he would leave the room. After about an hour the POW would be taken back to his cell to wonder again when the ax would really fall. The POWs did not submit until the actual beating and torture took place.

After all had "surrendered" they were allowed to live together in Room 3 of the Stables. Of course, none of the POWs really submitted to Fidel. They told him they did only when forced to do so.

Fidel told the men that they would now receive better treatment. They were allowed to do yard work and received four cigarettes a day. They made wooden toys for children. They began to receive mail from home and were allowed to write once a month. However, during this time daily beatings of one or all of these were common. Fidel introduced the rubber fan belt for whippings.

One of the POWs in the Fidel group was treated with unmerciful brutality. Eric had been badly beaten and tortured at "Heartbreak Hotel" before being placed into Fidel's hands. The torture had apparently been allowed to go too far and Eric was no longer rational by the time he arrived at the Zoo. He would fantasize and project himself out of the real world. He would not bow to or even acknowledge the presence of Fidel or any of the Vietnamese. No amount of beating or torture would make him respond. He trusted no one, not even the POWs. Fidel would beat Eric until he was near death and would still get no response.

The nine men in the Stables had to force-feed Eric to keep him alive. Finally the Vietnamese took him away from Fidel and attempted to give him medical help, including electric shock treatments, in an effort to save him. He was seen on occasion and was thought to be living solo. He was last seen alive in December of 1970. The POWs were later told by the Vietnamese that Eric had died.

In the summer of 1968, the Vietnamese were working on Jim Kasler to get him to talk to a delegation, but were unsuccessful. Jim was one of the true heroes among the POWs. The first time I saw him I thought he was dead. I was looking out the crack of the door in Cell Six of the Pigsty when two guards came by carrying a stretcher with Jim on it. His face was ashen. A couple of months later I saw him walking very slowly on crutches. Directly behind Jim was an armed guard with a bayonet pointed at his back. He took a lot of torture and abuse from the Vietnamese and was a source of inspiration for the rest of us.

Fidel decided to help the Vietnamese to get Jim to see a delegation. Fidel used ropes and irons in eleven torture sessions. Fidel then resorted to beatings, denial of sleep, and a starvation diet. Jim surrendered a number of times, but when the Vietnamese tried to get him to prepare to see the delegation, usually the day after surrendering, Jim would tell them to "cram it." Fidel would then start a new series of torture. Jim was bedridden for six months following the torture.

The Fidel program lasted for about one year. Fidel and Chico were not seen after August 1968.

Beginning in late 1967, the Vietnamese initiated what was commonly called the "Quiz-Kid Program." After attending English classes, some young noncommissioned Vietnamese were selected to remain in camp, and these "Quiz Kids" held quiz after quiz with some of the POWs. The purpose of the quizzes seemed to be twofold. First, they provided an opportunity for them to improve their English, and second, there was the ever-present propaganda program. The Quiz Kids soon started helping the officers with their programs and later they assumed some responsibility for the buildings, but still under one of the lower ranking camp officers. The Quiz Kids later served more as turnkeys and were with the POWs until release in 1973.

I had only one quiz with them, probably because I never argued or discussed anything with any of the Vietnamese personnel.

One day I was in the shower room washing my clothes when one of the Kiddies came in and began tapping out the code to Room 6. Fortunately the POWs in Room 6 did not respond. The Kiddy (we called him "The Teenager") smiled at me and departed.

North Vietnamese Army personnel administered the prison camps. Basically the same functions were performed at all the camps. Camp commanders were involved in administration and policy, although it was impossible to determine who dictated the overall treatment of POWs. The officers in charge of buildings were responsible for POW interrogation/indoctrination and treatment. In the early days the turnkeys meted out most of the day-to-day punishment, but after 1969 had little authority. Their main responsibility was to tend to daily needs of the POWs. Armed guards patrolled the grounds and manned the towers.

We attempted to standardize the names we had for all the enemy personnel. The Vietnamese officers and guards occasionally moved from one camp to another, and thus would have more than one name.

Some of the Vietnamese officers' names were: J.C.; Dum Dum; Rabbit; Bug; Frenchy; Spot; Chester; the Paper Boy; Elf; Rabies; Rat; Fox; Goldie; Stag; Soft Soap Fairy; and Lump (the only civilian in the camp, believed to be a political man).

Some of the guards' names were: Frog; A.B.; Snake; Ichabod; McGoo; Joe Louis; Husky.

The female soldiers (chow girls) were: Nightmare Alice; Gravel Gertie.

There was also "The Goon Squad," a group of soldiers who did most of the more serious forms of torture.

I even had names for the lizards that lived in our cell: Long-Tail Mama; Short-Tail Mama; Big Daddy; and the Acrobat, a young one that was always being tossed off the walls by the bigger lizards.

Things quieted down somewhat for us after October. The communications purge seemed to have reached all the buildings in the "Zoo," and we had lost contact with some of them.

FROM THE DUNGEONS OF NORTH VIETNAM

On Christmas Eve Bob, Tom, and I were taken to view a tree the Vietnamese had decorated. We were given some candy and extra cigarettes to take back to our room. Later in the evening we heard a guard opening the hatches to each of the cells. When he came to our cell he asked, "Protestant or Catholic?" We told him we were Protestants and he gave us each a small bag that contained an orange, several cookies, and small pieces of candy. This was our first "gift from the priest." We found out later that the Catholics received a tangerine instead of an orange. (Only the Lord knows why!) One POW who was living by himself told the guard that he was neither Protestant nor Catholic. The guard closed the hatch without giving him anything. Next Christmas he decided to be a Protestant!

Some Christmas music was played over the camp radio. We also had to listen to a tape recording by a Vietnamese Catholic priest who told us to pray to God for forgiveness of our crimes against the Vietnamese people.

It was a quiet evening for us as we reminisced about our families and other Christmases. Our prayers were for those POWs who were still in irons or in solitary confinement, and for those suffering from wounds.

Christmas day we had a good dinner of meat, vegetables, and rice. In quantity it was about the size of an average American meal, but about six times our normal ration.

Three or four times in early 1968 we were taken to the auditorium to see propaganda movies, usually documentaries of the Vietnamese version of how the war was being won. We sat on the floor, and blankets were used as curtains to separate the POWs. I would touch the POW next to me through the blanket and tap messages to him. One day I attempted communicating by tapping on a foot and immediately received a hard slap across my head. It was a guard's foot!

There were at least two rooms in the auditorium that were being used to torture POWs. Our attempts to communicate with them failed.

For three days one week we were taken outside and told to make coal balls from coal dust and water. We did this gladly because the coal was used to cook our food. In fact, we would have loved to work in the garden or pull weeds or do things that would be beneficial to us. Just being out in the fresh air would be great.

Another major camp shuffle of POWs took place in March 1968. Bob, Tom, and I were moved to Room 2 of the Stables, next door to the Fidel group. We established communications with them and asked Al if the SRO had any orders or guidelines for us. Al said that the SRO had been tortured so badly that he would not give any more orders. He said that he just could not take any more torture.

The Snake, alias "Old Incredible," was our new turnkey. Al told us that the Snake was one of the meanest and most sadistic of the enemy. We found out how true that was a few days later. Tom was the first of us to get hit by the Snake. Tom bowed with a cigarette in his mouth. He was forced to kneel down and was slapped two or three times. One day, while we were outside bathing, I was kicked in my hip. No apparent reason.

Bob, being the SRO of our cell, took the brunt of Snake's wrath. Almost every day one of us was beaten or slapped. On Easter Sunday the Snake decided to teach me how to bow. He came to me and said, "Bow." I gave my usual nod and he hit me with his fist. He grabbed me by the arm and slung me outside the cell. Two more guards came running up and began beating Bob and Tom. The Snake continued hitting me about the head and kicking me. I rolled with the punches as much as possible. His next to last punch was a karate chop to the back of my neck that sent me to the floor. He yelled "Bow!" I struggled to my feet and bowed. He hit me across the head one more time and then sent me back to the cell. The other guards finished with Bob and Tom and sent them to the cell also. They left us alone for several days, but then the Snake continued as usual.

I was outside washing my clothes one afternoon and I saw Fidel and the Lump walk by. Fidel stopped abruptly and glared at me. He seemed confused as to who I was. I bowed and he immediately walked away in the direction he had arrived. Bob was of the opinion that we were being groomed to join the Fidel program. I disagreed, not only because of Fidel's reaction when he saw me, but also because POWs were still being moved from cell to cell. I thought we were just temporarily parked in the Stables.

I began to have doubts, though, as the days dragged on. I really dreaded to get up in the mornings, wondering if I was going to be beaten or worse. I regained my courage at night but it would begin to wane as daylight approached. I could still sleep only a few minutes at a time. Then I would have to rub my legs and hip until the pain eased somewhat.

One day while Bob was being worked over by the Snake, I prayed, "Dear God, how much longer are You going to put up with this?" As it turned out that was the last time the Snake beat on us. I often thought about prayer during those days. I realized that every time I had prayed for courage, I received courage. Many times I said a prayer that went like this: "Dear God, please give me the courage to do what I have to do or say what I have to say." It always worked.

As things slacked off we relaxed somewhat and played word games in the evenings. "Ghost" was our favorite. One of us would think of a word and say the first letter. The next man would say another letter, possibly thinking of a different word. The game proceeded thusly until someone could not think of a word with that particular series of letters. He could fake it if he wished but would probably get challenged, and if he were wrong would receive a "g." The first man to get to "ghost" would lose the game.

The Tet Offensive was the big news in the first few months of 1968. I had a quiz with the Elf (the ugliest little man I have ever seen!), who told me that the Vietnamese liberation fighters were pushing the U.S. into the sea. The war would be over soon and many POWs would be going home. I said nothing.

In conjunction with Tet (Vietnamese New Year) the Vietnamese released three POWs to a delegation from the United States. The Vietnamese attempted to use this release as an example to prove to the POWs that their fate was indeed in the hands of the Vietnamese. For the most part, it had no big effect upon our attitudes, other than disappointment in the behavior of the releasees.

In late April I was taken out of the Stables and moved to another building, the "Pool Hall." I stayed there one week with Ken. We were then moved to a camp next to the Zoo that I had named the "Annex."

THE ANNEX

Seventy-one POWs moved into the Annex. We were all junior officers, that is, captains and lieutenants, except for three enlisted men. The camp consisted of five buildings with two cells in each building. Our cell was twenty-one feet long by twenty feet wide. The beds were made of wooden boards with no legs. I lived with eight other men. Robert was the SRO.

Communications were established between all cells and buildings within a few weeks, but it was difficult communicating between the Annex and the Zoo. A wall separated the two camps. One of our cells was in sight of a building in the Zoo, but communications could be established only during outside time, and usually the guards were around. Initially we had a problem discerning who the Annex SRO was. A Navy lieutenant knew that he had been promoted to lieutenant commander and that the promotion had become effective after he had been shot down. Eventually we received orders from the Zoo that we would use the date of rank we had when we were shot down to determine camp and building SROs. This was the rule throughout all camps until some modifications were made in 1971.

Peace negotiations began in May and optimism was rampant throughout the camp. There was a dramatic improvement in our living conditions. Diet was better. Sometimes we had bread instead of rice. Living in a nine-man room aided greatly in morale, organizations, and resistance postures. Each cell had a walled-in courtyard and we were allowed to stay outside for one hour each day except Sunday. There was some improvement in medical treatment. Sometimes aspirin was available.

Chow was brought to us in huge pails and we would dish it up ourselves, as opposed to previous years when the guards did this for us. Each of us received one and one-half loaves of bread along with the usual bowl of soup. The soup varied during this period— squash, turnip, cabbage, and sometimes bean broth, as well as the standard greens. Glenn tried to fatten me by giving me some of his bread each meal.

Many POWs thought we would be home within one year. I made the prophetic announcement: "Across the Sea in Seventy-three" and was roundly booed!

Periodically we gained some extra time outside by sweeping, pulling weeds, and fertilizing gardens inside the camp.

Cell inspections were held each week. We had to stand facing the wall with hands up until the inspection was over.

The old issue of digging foxholes came up again. Same arguments, pro and con. The Annex SRO issued orders to refuse to dig foxholes. Some POWs were asked by the Vietnamese to dig, but they refused and nothing more was said.

Well water was used for bathing. A bucket was tied to a long rope and we would haul the water up. Occasionally someone would drop the rope and it would fall ten to fifteen feet into the well. We would then call out, "Bao cao" (Vietnamese term for assistance). The guard would bring a hook to fish it out. There was also an outhouse in the courtyard in addition to the waste bucket inside the cell.

Walking around inside our room was our main exercise. Some of the men jogged in place and did sit-ups and pushups. I could do a few of each, but no jogging. My legs began to get stronger from the increased amount of exercise.

It is important to note that the inter- and intra-camp moves meant so much to the POWs. Reasons for shuffles were rather obscure and seemed self-defeating when the Vietnamese efforts to deny communications between POWs were considered. These shuffles brought men together from different cells and camps, and so we were able to exchange considerable information. We learned of camps called Plantation and Farnsworth and Briarpatch and Son Tay, and the names of some buildings associated with the Hanoi Hilton—Little Vegas, New Guy Village, Alcatraz, and Skid Row.

In July 1968, another group of POWs was released. The release was exploited by the Vietnamese through a program in which they actively tried to recruit a large number of POWs for release in the near future. The Vietnamese wanted to get letters from POWs requesting amnesty. This letter was necessary because no one would go home without writing for amnesty. They said that each POW who had been released had written one. A few POWs wrote the letters and the Vietnamese used them for propaganda. Later, when these POWs were being pressed for propaganda, the Vietnamese would threaten them with exposure of the letters to all POWs and the world. I was never asked to write such a letter.

Paul asked me one day if I would go home early. I said, "Paul, one of these days someone, probably my son, will ask me how I did as a POW. I want to be able to look him in the eye and say, 'I did the best I could.' No, Paul, I will not go home early. When I return, it will be with honor."

Paul was nearly blind from some kind of disease. The Vietnamese would not give him any medical treatment. He and J.B. had been shot down in 1965 and had lived together most of the time. They had moved next door to George and me in the Pigsty and had taught us the tap code. J.B. was our room's representative from the Navy.

Neil had been shot down about three months before I had. His left arm had been broken just below the shoulder. After the cast was removed he was tortured for something and the arm was again broken. They had not bothered to reset or recast the arm. The bone was completely broken and his arm was simply hanging by skin and muscle. He had lost all feeling in his hand and fingers and could not move them. Somewhere Neil had found a string that he had tied around his neck to hold his arm up and protect it somewhat. We took turns massaging his arm. One day he and I were standing in the open doorway. I had been giving him a massage when all at once Robert came charging by on his way to bathe. Robert slipped and began falling down the steps leading to the courtyard. Instinctively I grabbed him with my left hand. Neil said, "Ted! Ted! My arm, my arm!" I realized I was holding on to Robert and Neil at the same time. I had given him an uncalled-for arm stretching!

Sometime later I was rubbing his arm and noticed tears in his eyes. I asked him what was wrong. He said, "I can move one of my fingers. Look!"

July and August were hot, miserable months. John, Glenn, and I went into hibernation as far as exercising was concerned. I picked up my first case of heat rash, and any type of exertion made it worse. I continued walking because it meant so much to me to try to get my legs back in shape. The hip hurt so badly. I still had visions of attempting an escape, but was grudgingly admitting to myself that in my physical condition survival would be impossible.

We had long discussions concerning escape. The odds were tremendously against a successful escape and evasion. Even if we could scrounge some basic survival equipment and keep them hidden until the right time, get out of the camp unnoticed, where would we go? To the South were hundreds of miles of heavily populated flatland. To the West were the Red River Valley and mountains and jungles. North was more mountains and Red China. Possibly a slim chance existed to the East, where one might make it to the South China Sea, steal a boat, and paddle or motor a few hundred miles, looking for a friendly Navy vessel. Some of us, myself included, thought it would be worth the effort to try to get a list of names out and to let the world know how we were being treated.

As the Christmas season of 1968 approached, some men were asked to go downtown Hanoi to attend Catholic or Protestant services. Most refused, some went. The issue was strongly debated in individual cells, but no orders or policies were set by the camp SRO. Some cell SROs left it up to the individual. Some thought it would be a good opportunity to receive information from other camps. No one in our cell went.

Even though peace negotiations had begun in Paris, our high hopes for an early settlement had vanished. We had continued our "Home for Christmas" prayer. One day one of the men said, "What will we do if we are not home for Christmas?" Someone answered, "We will continue to pray for next Christmas."

As the season grew nearer the men began writing down the words for holiday songs. We used toilet paper, pens made from strips of bamboo, and ink from a mixture of cigarette ashes and water. Of course we kept these carefully hidden from our captors.

Neil received a package from home. He shared everything with the rest of us. What a wonderful treat! Actual goodies from home!

Again we received a "gift from the priest."

I shall never forget that Christmas Eve. A group of men quietly singing such carols as "Hark, The Herald Angels Sing" and "Silent Night." Before retiring, Jim said, "Everyone who believes in Santa Claus, hang a stocking on your mosquito net. Remember, those who believe will receive!"

I did not hang up a sock because I needed to wear them to try to keep warm. We each had two thin blankets, but I had to use one of mine as a cushion for my bad hip.

In the quiet of the night, as I had done the two previous Christmas Eves, I mentally shopped for, bought, and wrapped gifts for Ruth and Kevin. *How are they? Are they well? Please, God, let them live normal and happy lives, and know that my thoughts are with them. May God bless and keep them, as well as the other members of the great Ballard family.*

When I awakened the next morning I found a Christmas card inside my net. The other men had one in their stockings. Jim had made them without any of us knowing about it!

More packages from home began arriving in January 1969. A receipt was required to be signed which contained a propaganda statement saying that we have received "humane and lenient treatment." This issue was hotly debated in most cells and caused ill feelings. I argued against signing the statement. I did not want to give them anything to use for propaganda purposes and thought that if we all refused to sign, the Vietnamese would take the controversial statement out. Nine men in the cell next to ours refused to sign. I was the only one in our cell to refuse. (Paul Kari told me he would not sign the statement, but he never received a package from home. His wife had divorced him after he was shot down.) Ken North, a friend of mine who lived in the Zoo, was tortured until he signed. John told me he would not sign; however, he came back from quiz one day with a package. He sat down next to me and said that he was sorry that he did not have the courage of his convictions. I told John not to worry about it. I thought that he could not take any more torture. His ankles and wrists had deep permanent scars from leg irons and wrist irons. He was thinner than I.

The SRO of the Zoo sent out word that it was okay to sign the receipt, that the U.S. government wanted us to have the packages, and that it was good for our morale.

I was the last person in our cell to be offered a package. I was taken to the quiz room and shown a package from Ruth. I recognized Ruth's handwriting on the address label. I had such a good feeling when I saw her name, and at the same time I almost cried. The Vietnamese had obviously removed most of the items. There was some toothpaste, candy, a magnetic chess set, and a pair of bedroom-type slippers. I really wanted those slippers. The rubber thongs that I wore were warped and hurt my feet and legs to walk in them. The officer asked if I wanted the package and I said, "Yes." He then said that I must sign a receipt. I said, "Okay." He handed me a sheet of paper that had all the items listed on it. At the top of the paper was a statement to the effect that the undersigned had received humane and lenient treatment. I told the officer that I would sign a receipt but would not sign the propaganda statement. He said I must sign the entire statement. I refused. He said that I could not have the package and for me to go back to my room. I said, "May I look at the contents one more time?" He said, "Yes." I looked at the items and the address label for a few moments and then left the room. I was amazed that I was not even threatened with punishment. The officer acted as if he couldn't care less whether I took the package.

All the men who received packages shared them with the rest of us. I felt uncomfortable about accepting the shared items, but I did not want to start any more arguments. Anyway, I thought that most of the men respected my decision and my courage.

When the next group of packages arrived (during the Christmas season), the propaganda statement was not part of the receipt.

The security of the camp was fairly lax in the spring of 1969. There were some holes in the outside walls. There were only two guards at night and when it was raining they huddled by the main gate and did not come around to check the cells. So we were not surprised when we received word from the Annex SRO that an escape attempt would be made soon. By this time I had doubts about an attempt. It seemed futile. I assumed the attempt would be made on a rainy Saturday night, because usually the guards left us alone on Sundays. They would not even get a head count.

Sure enough, on Sunday morning, May 10, we received a message that two men, Captains Ed Atterbury and John Dramesi from Cell Six, had left the building around midnight the night before. Robert and J.B. were ashen-faced at this news. They knew from experience that the Vietnamese would react harshly to such action.

Later that day we received word that the two men had been recaptured and had been brought to the Zoo. As the news filtered through the camp, a feeling of helpless frustration settled over all the POWs. Each man tried to prepare himself mentally as best he could for the expected crackdown.

The remaining seven men from Cell Six were split up and isolated in several cells in the Annex and Zoo, where they were subjected to an intense torture program that was to last two weeks.

Sunday evening two guards came into our cell, looked around, and removed a pair of tennis shoes that Paul had been given when he was captured in 1965.

The initial reaction of the Vietnamese camp personnel to the escape was one of dazed unbelief for the first two or three days. They could not seem to believe that anyone could or would try to escape, possibly because the Paris Peace Talks had just started, and also because they thought their camp security was superb. Camp routine seemed to be normal on Monday morning except that the guards were very serious. There was usually some degree of chatter among them that was missing. On Wednesday, a thorough inspection of the Annex and the Zoo was made by unfamiliar Vietnamese under the supervision of high-ranking staff officers. All materials of any kind that could possibly be used in an escape were taken. Each cell was checked for security.

At the end of the first two weeks the remaining seven men from Cell Six were put back together in Cell Nine and placed in leg irons. The Annex SRO and the SROs from all the other cells in the camp were removed from these cells. The Annex SRO was taken to the Hanoi Hilton and did not return until October 1969. When Robert was taken from our cell, we stood up and silently prayed for God to give him courage.

Bob and the other cell SROs were isolated in the Zoo, where they also endured an intensive torture program that lasted two weeks. One of the escapees, Ed Atterbury, died from the torture. Eugene (Red) McDaniel, an SRO, came close to dying. He received over nine hundred lashes from a rubber fan belt. One of his arms was broken. Several men attempted suicide but, fortunately, were stopped in time by the guards.

Immediate steps were taken to prevent another escape. The broken lights on the perimeter wall were replaced. The trees in the courtyard were cut down. A guard tower was built in the southwest corner of the camp. The guards checked the cells several times each night.

The wall vents were bricked up and the air holes in the ceilings were covered, cutting off all air circulation in the cells. The bed boards were removed and we had to sleep on the floor. Outside time was cut and was generally limited to one wash period per day. This varied with cells. The men in leg irons were allowed out only once per week.

As the Vietnamese gained more and more information from the tortured POWs, a strong effort was made to stop all communications. Mats were put in all the back air vents of the two buildings (the Barn and the Garage) adjoining the Annex. All holes in the courtyard were plugged.

The camp officials were embarrassed by the escape and were determined to get revenge. They implemented a program of strict discipline and harassment. Harsh punishment was in store for any violation of camp regulations. Complete silence was demanded and enforced during outside periods. One man was beaten several times across the legs with a fan belt because he dropped his dish while washing it. Ken was given fifteen lashes for sleeping in the nude. Glenn was given six lashes for calling a guard an SOB. Glenn had some problems with his gums and had asked the guard for an aspirin. The guard refused.

A few weeks after the escape a group of camp officials went to each cell, had the POWs line up in the courtyard, then read them their punishment for violating the camp regulations during the escape. The punishment varied between cells but in general was a cutting-off of cigarettes and bathing for two weeks.

Efforts were also undertaken to reduce POW physical capabilities to the point where escape would be impossible. We were not allowed to exercise in any manner or even to walk around in our cell. The quantity and quality of food were reduced. Very little protein, such as fish, pork fat, or soybean curd, was put in our diet. Much harassment and trouble were caused by the no-exercise policy because all the POWs who were physically able had always exercised daily to some extent. In addition, walking was an excellent means to pass the time as well as a good form of exercise.

The building and cell SROs and other senior POWs all received major torture to divulge communications links and procedures, camp organization, committees, etc. They were tortured to confirm information that had been gained from other POWs. Some false information had been given to stop the torture. When this was discovered, the torture became more and more brutal. Torture sessions lasted from one to two weeks, or longer in some cases. The methods used included beatings, irons, ropes, sleep deprivation, no food or water, kneeling for long periods, and being hoisted by the feet and dropped on the head.

The Vietnamese began having the POWs fill out biographical forms. J.B. was tortured to do so. He was now our cell SRO and told the rest of us to fill the forms out as long as we did not give any new information. Paul was beaten because he could not see the form well enough to fill it out. I told the same lies as before about not being married.

J.B. was removed from our cell in late July. About a week later Jim, John, Ken, and I were moved to another cell in the Annex to live with Bill, Jimmy, Jay, and Mike.

Jim was our cell SRO, with Jay second in command. Jimmy was in leg irons. It was amazing to watch him get in and out of his pajamas. The guards thought he had picked the lock until he showed them how he did it. He could do leg lifts with the irons on.

We were required to keep our clothing and thongs aligned a certain way during the ongoing purge. One day the Squirt, one of the quiz kids, did not like the way my thongs were aligned and told me to kneel down. I told him that I could not because of my bad hip. He insisted and I continued to refuse. This continued for a few moments with the Squirt threatening punishment. Suddenly I noticed a Vietnamese in civilian clothing standing in the courtyard. He called the Squirt outside. When the Squirt came back inside the cell he told me to obey the camp regulations, closed the door, and left. About that time I remembered who the man was. He was the man who had called himself the camp commander and had supervised my torture in the Green Room, some three years earlier.

The results of the summer-long purge and their effects on the POWs were of great importance. Many men had undergone brutal torture, resulting in all POW camp information being divulged to the Vietnamese. Much propaganda material was obtained. Some POWs were forced to write letters requesting amnesty and to make other statements during their torture sessions.

Before the escape we had to listen to the "Voice of Vietnam" radio broadcast twice each day. After the escape, some POWs were forced to read articles from a Vietnamese newspaper that were taped and played over the camp radio. The "Voice of Vietnam" was never heard again in the Annex.

In early September 1969, we were told to put on our long clothing and sit around the camp radio. We were told to sit at attention, listen carefully, and not to talk. The Vietnamese then announced that their president, Ho Chi Minh, had died.

A national thirty-day mourning period went into effect. All Vietnamese guards and officers wore black armbands or a black ribbon. There was virtually no camp activity for the first week or so except the necessities of daily living. There was a constant daily barrage of radio broadcasts about Ho Chi Minh's life. We had to put on our long clothes and sit down while the radio was playing. We were told by the officers to be very careful of our actions because the guards were very sad and might react with violence if aroused.

During the second week in October the men who were in irons in Cell Eight had a quiz with the "Fox," who had just taken over as camp commander. They were informed that their punishment was over. Their leg irons were removed and they returned to their cell. This signaled a complete change in POW treatment. At about the same time the senior POWs in the Zoo were taken out of irons and allowed to live with other POWs.

The guards slowly eased their constant harassment, and over the following weeks, many of the most sadistic were replaced. I never again saw the Frog, the Snake, or McGoo.

Our cell vents were opened and the bed boards were returned along with a wooden bench for each cell. Each man received an extra mat and blanket and a new, large, colorful, striped towel. Outside time was increased and restraints on making noise were lifted. Punishment during the first three or four months of this period was to confine a man to his cell during the outside time.

The Vietnamese gave the men cards and chess sets that had been taken from previous packages. They also gave out two quick rounds of packages in October and December. We were allowed to write a letter home. A few refused for personal reasons but the majority wrote a six-line letter, highly censored by the Vietnamese, then recopied on a standard letterform. I had about eight hundred million things I wanted to say to Ruth and questions to ask. I started out, "Dear sister Ruth..." I asked about "Cousin" Kevin. I had given this false information to my captors after being tortured.

In November our cigarette ration was increased from three to six. Three of the men in our cell did not smoke, so we usually had plenty of cigarettes. They were locally made and tough tasting. Occasionally we would be taken off cigarettes for a week or so. I would miss them for a couple of days; then it would not bother me.

Despite an overwhelming sense of relief that the pressures and tensions had finally eased, our initial reaction to the change in treatment was one of suspicion. Experience had shown that the

Vietnamese could not be trusted. There were several possible reasons for the change. Some felt that Ho Chi Minh had been responsible for our harsh treatment, and his death allowed the Vietnamese leaders to change that policy. However, most of us thought that the Paris Peace Talks, along with the fact that we were a powerful bargaining tool, made the difference. Our survival had taken on an added importance to the Vietnamese.

Several of us received packages from home, which we shared. I was thankful that the "humane and lenient" statement was no longer included in the receipt.

In my package was a set of thermal underwear, for which I was most grateful. Jimmy had insisted that I take one of his blankets, and now, finally, I could at least stay warm on those long, sleepless, miserable nights.

During the week before Christmas a number of men from the camp (mostly Catholic) were selected to attend church services at a church in Hanoi. No one in our cell was asked. We discussed it and had decided that we would not go if asked. This turned out to be a massive propaganda program for the Vietnamese. The entire service was filmed and taped. Another group was taken to Protestant services in the Zoo, where contact was made with the Zoo POWs and communications procedures were arranged.

We made Christmas cards for the men in the other buildings. These were "air-mailed" by tying a rock to the papers and throwing them from our courtyard to theirs.

For a Christmas tree, we decorated a small Swiss-type broom with strips of cloth and paper with various designs. Mike was quite a good artist and enjoyed doing things with his hands. He used one of his black pajama tops as a background and drew a tree on it. From paper and cloth he made stars and other ornaments and attached them to the tree. Small packages with each of our names were also attached. This was hidden during the day but was hung on the wall in the evenings for our enjoyment.

We exchanged gifts that Christmas, both real and imaginary. I gave away gift certificates and treated everyone to a dinner at the Fireside Inn in Las Vegas. One man, who had lost most of his hair, was given a wooden comb. I was given earplugs and a nose clip so I would not be disturbed at night by nearby neighbors!

Christmas Eve the guards came around and gave us the "gift from the priest" and cookies and cigarettes. We were in a good mood and talked and quietly sang carols till fairly late.

Before retiring we each tied a stocking to our nets. I had saved some peanut butter candy from my package Ruth had sent and planned to put some in each man's stocking while they were asleep. I lay awake for about an hour and was just about ready to get up when I heard a noise and looked up. A POW was putting something in my stocking. He moved quickly from net to net and then sneaked back under his own. Ten minutes later another man got up and did the same thing. It took almost two hours for all eight of us to play Santa Claus.

Early Christmas morning I was awakened by a loud shout from Jimmy: "Merry Christmas, everybody! Get up! He did it—Santa Claus came! He did it! Get up! Get up!"

What a sight—Jimmy running from net to net, pulling everybody out of bed, exuberant as a small child. Our stockings were full of candy, gifts, and greeting cards.

Later that day, the turnkey discovered the "pajama top" Christmas tree and took it away. That evening Mike was taken to quiz. The officers had Mike's artwork spread out on the table and were admiring it. The Fox told Mike that they were going to take his work to the Art Museum downtown. Mike said, "No, you are not," picked up the shirt, ripped it, and tore everything off it. An irate Fox threatened punishment and sent Mike back to his cell. Nothing else came of the incident.

In January, many men began receiving letters from home. They were not allowed to keep the letters. They read them and gave them back to the Vietnamese officers.

In February some high-ranking officials came to each cell and informed us that we no longer had to bow. Instead, we need only to stand at attention and nod our heads in greeting. This was a pleasant surprise, and a long-awaited event for us all. Shortly after this, Chester and Joe Louis started a program to have us lean forward fifteen degrees and then nod the head. At quiz one day I refused to do this, saying that the gesture was degrading and insulting. I had to stand in the corner for five minutes!

Eventually, in early summer, the head nod was eliminated and the only requirement was to stand.

One night everyone in our cell was taken to the administrative building and told to put on some civilian clothes, that we were going to visit the Army Art Museum. They said we needed to be in civilian clothes so that the Vietnamese people would not recognize us as POWs—they were very angry with us. All of us refused to put on the clothes or leave the camp. They did not seem surprised at our refusal and sent us back to our cell.

PART ONE: IN THE DUNGEONS

The period from January to August 1970 saw a general increase in Vietnamese attempts to give us better treatment. Packages and letters arrived more frequently, the quality of food increased somewhat, and harassment became almost nonexistent. No case of brutality or strong physical pressure was reported.

One day I was taken to quiz. I sat on a stool in front of Chester, who appeared to be reading a letter. He asked, "You are not married?"

I said, "No."

He asked, "Why not?"

I said, "Perhaps I am too ugly."

He looked at me, nodded, and said, "Perhaps you are right. You are not married?"

"No."

"You lie. I have a letter from a ten-year-old boy named Kevin who calls you 'Daddy.' What do you say now?"

I smiled to myself and said, "You are confused. He is my cousin. Let me read this letter and I will explain it to you."

"No. You will not receive any letters or packages until you tell the truth. Now go back to your room."

The next day I was taken back to quiz and was told that I must rewrite my biography and tell the truth or be severely punished. I told him that I had nothing new to add. He said, "You will be punished" and sent me back.

★ ★ 63 ★ ★

Later that week, Chester told me that I was very weak and thin. I agreed. He said that if I wished to receive some milk and extra meat, I would have to write a letter to the camp commander and request it. I said I would not write such a letter. He looked at me silently for a few moments. I said, "I will write a letter requesting that all POWs receive better food and medical treatment."

Chester said, "That is not possible. You will write for yourself?"

I said, "No."

"Go to your room."

At my next quiz, a few days later, the Fox told me to write a statement telling how I had been treated since being captured. He threatened punishment if I did not write. I wrote for about an hour, listing the bad things and nothing good. I told about my many torture sessions, the breaking of my hip, and the complete lack of medical attention. The Fox came back into the room and read the statement. He became furious and said I would be tortured if I did not strike out the bit about the broken hip.

I said, "You will torture me?" This was the first time he had used the word "torture."

He yelled, "You will be tortured!"

I scratched out the bit about the broken hip.

After talking my situation over with my cellmates, I decided to tell the truth about my marriage. I asked Chester if I could now receive the letters from my wife and son and also the packages that had been denied me. He said I would receive them after I had rewritten my biography, which would be done later.

Every meal, for about a two-week period, we received Irish potatoes. Jim was taken to quiz and was asked how he liked the food. Jim told the officer that the food had improved somewhat. He was asked what kind of food he would like. Jim said, "How about some sweet potatoes for a change?" The officer nodded. Sure enough, the next day we received sweet potatoes—Irish potatoes with sugar on them!

In early August 1970, the first indication of a possible move was sensed when the Vietnamese removed the bed boards from all cells. About ten men moved out of camp. On 20 August the remaining fifty-six of us were loaded on buses and taken to a camp called Camp Faith. As far as we know the Annex was closed on that night and was never again used to house American POWs.

CAMP FAITH

Camp Faith was roughly twenty miles west of Hanoi and consisted of six separate compounds. Our compound was separated from the one south of us by a wall. We had no contact with the other four compounds, which were several hundred yards to the west. There were five cells in one long building. I lived in a twelve-man cell along with the compound SRO, Captain Konrad Troutman. Konnie had been the SRO of the Annex and had been severely tortured after the escape attempt.

We were allowed outside to bathe and exercise twice each day, one cell at a time. There was now open communication between all cells. We passed notes covertly to the compound next door. The officers and guards seemed to feel insecure with so many POWs in contact with each other, so they kept a wary eye on us.

Our bathing area was under a shed and consisted of a large tank that was kept full of water by a continuously running faucet. The tank was about fifteen feet long, four feet wide, and four feet high. We would dip pails into the tank and pour the water over our bodies. The outside privy was made up of five separate stalls.

All things considered, our living conditions had improved greatly. However, we were back to eating rice and mostly greens soup. The Vietnamese began building an outside stove in which they said we would be baking our own bread. I was looking forward to that.

We began clearing an oval-shaped track for the men to run or jog around.

My physical condition had improved a little. My legs still hurt so badly that I could not get much sleep at night. I continued walking every day as I had done ever since the cast was removed from my leg nearly four years earlier. I walked until I could stand it no longer. Then I would sit or lie down and rub my legs. When the pain eased I would walk some more. One day I told Glenn Nix that I was going to start a running program; that I would either ruin my legs completely or make them better. Glenn agreed but advised a cautious approach. As soon as we were outside again I jogged for about ten yards. I walked for a few yards, then jogged ten more. The pain did not seem to increase much, so I thought I was doing the right thing. Gradually, over the next few months, I could feel myself getting stronger even though the pain persisted. By the time we were released in early 1973, I could jog about a mile.

After we had been at Camp Faith for a few weeks, all fifty-six of us were allowed outside at the same time. I suggested to Konnie that we act more militarily and initiate a saluting program. This caused a sometimes-heated debate. Some POWs felt that we should postpone such action because of our improved treatment. They did not want to raise the ire of the guards. Some liked the idea; they would do anything to aggravate the Vietnamese. Konnie finally gave out orders for the SRO of each cell to report to him each day and salute. The officers threatened torture. We continued saluting. Eventually, even the Vietnamese were acting more like soldiers, and began saluting each other!

Tom McNish was a big man from North Carolina—about six feet, two inches tall, and strong as a bull. One evening he accidentally bent one of the bars in their window and was accused of attempting to escape. He was put in solitary confinement, in leg irons, in a small room at one end of the building. His cellmates passed him a message that they were going to name the room "Uncle Tom's Cabin." Tom screamed bloody murder! The Vietnamese forgave him of his "crimes against the people" after about a week.

The Elf told me that I must rewrite my biography and tell the absolute truth. I rewrote it, giving the new information about being married. I then asked for the letters and packages that had been withheld. The Elf said, "Maybe later."

On 27 October, 1970, Kevin's birthday, I received my first letter from Ruth. Four years, one month, and one day after being shot down. There was a snapshot of Ruth and one of Kevin. I wish I could describe my feelings. I cannot.

A few days later I wrote my second letter home. In it I asked Ruth to send some vitamins, pipe tobacco, honey, and Knox gelatin. George McSwain had discovered that the gelatin helped get rid of heat rash.

I was pleased to be living in the same cell with my good friend Glenn Nix once again. Glenn meant a great deal to me. He and John Brodak were two of the most intelligent men I had ever known. Glenn was an extremely well-read individual and told us many stories when we had lived together in the Annex. He had learned to speak German from one of his earlier cellmates and had imparted his knowledge to us. I never could handle the grammar very well, but I had long vocabulary lists in my mind, which I had made using Harry Lorayne's memory technique. I taught this system to more than one hundred POWs in the next year or so, and it was an invaluable aid to us, not only academically but also in memorizing all POW names and orders from the SROs. It was an outstanding way to keep the mind active.

In November there was an unsuccessful attempt by the United States to rescue some POWs from a camp at Son Tay, which was located about seven miles from our camp. We heard the choppers, gunfire, and other noises and wondered what was going on. Within the next few days all of the POWs were moved to downtown Hanoi to a large complex of jails named Hoalo Prison. We called it the Hanoi Hilton. Finally, after so many years, we were all in the same camp, with twenty-five to fifty-six men per cell. We became better organized militarily, academically, and religiously.

PART
TWO

REFLECTIONS

CHRISTMAS IN THE DUNGEONS OF NORTH VIETNAM

Christmas, 1966

On December 24, 1966, I was living in a small twelve feet by twelve feet cell. My roommate was Navy Ensign George McSwain. We had no contact with other American POWs. For seven weeks, George had been undergoing a torture that was called "holding up the wall"—standing facing the wall with his arms straight over his head. Periodically the guards would come in and beat him up. The Vietnamese were torturing George in an attempt to get me to sign a war crimes confession. I will not go into any details, but earlier they had tortured me for the same thing and failed.

I had spent two months in a cast, from my left ankle to my chest, and was now using crutches to hobble around the room.

As evening approached, a guard came and took George to be interviewed by some Vietnamese officers. While he was gone I suddenly felt the urge to walk without the crutches. I carried them with me but did not use them and made it all the way around the room. I had given myself a Christmas present and waited impatiently for George to come back so I could share it with him.

When George returned he had a few pieces of sugar candy and a cigarette for each of us. This was a pleasant surprise since I never thought the Vietnamese would recognize Christmas. George said the quiz room was full of oranges and bananas and we would receive some later. We never did.

Later some Christmas music was played over the camp radio. A POW sang two or three songs. I wondered who he was but never did find out. It was a sad Christmas Eve for me. As we went to bed, George was silent and despondent. We did not talk as we normally did. I could only imagine his thoughts. Mine were of my family and Christmases past.

The gong did not clang as usual Christmas morning. However, a guard came by and told George to get "on the wall." About three hours later he was taken to quiz and the officer (whom we called Dum-dum) told him that the camp commander had forgiven him of his "crimes" and he must obey the camp regulations. We were both jubilant at this news.

George's long ordeal was over. In a way we felt it was a victory for us since I did not have to write a confession or condemn the United States government. Several times I came close to calling a halt to the torture and writing the statement, but George was a tough man and he took it as he said he could. The Vietnamese gave us a good Christmas dinner—a piece of meat, lots of rice, and, for the first time, cabbage soup.

Christmas 1967

The summer and fall of 1967 were a bad time for the POWs. Many men were tortured for propaganda purposes, and harassment by the guards was continuous.

PART TWO: REFLECTIONS

There were about thirty men in our building, three to each room. My cellmates were Captain Bob Sandvick and Captain Tom Pyle.

On Christmas Eve we were taken to view a tree the Vietnamese had decorated. We were given some candy and extra cigarettes to take back to our rooms. Later in the evening we heard a guard opening the hatches to each of the cells. When he came to our cell he asked, "Protestant or Catholic?" We told him we were Protestants and he gave us each a small bag, which contained an orange, several cookies, and small pieces of candy. This was our first "gift from the priest." We found out later that the Catholics got a tangerine instead of an orange. (Only the Lord knows why!) One POW who was living by himself told the guard he was neither Protestant nor Catholic. The guard closed the hatch without giving him anything! Next Christmas he decided to be a Protestant!

Some Christmas music was played over the camp radio. We also had to listen to a tape recording by a Vietnamese Catholic priest. He allowed that we should pray to God for forgiveness of our crimes against the Vietnamese people.

Bob, Tom, and I reminisced about our families and other Christmases. It was a quiet evening for us. Our prayers were for those POWs who were still suffering from wounds.

Christmas Day we had a good dinner of meat, vegetables, and rice. In quantity it was about the size of an average American meal, but about six times our normal ration.

The senior ranking officer of our building initiated a "Home for Christmas" prayer. Each day at noon a signal was passed to all rooms. We would then recite the Lord's Prayer.

Christmas, 1968

In the spring of 1968, I was moved to another camp. Living conditions were somewhat improved. There were nine of us in a twenty-one by twenty-foot room. Even though harassment and treatment by the guards were about the same, it was great to have more Americans to talk with. Peace negotiations had begun in Paris, but by the time Christmas came around, our high hopes for an early settlement had vanished.

We had continued our daily "Home for Christmas" prayer. One day one of the men said, "What will we do if we don't make it home for Christmas?" Someone answered, "We will continue to pray for next Christmas."

As the season grew nearer the men began writing down the words for holiday songs. We used toilet paper, pens made from strips of bamboo, and ink from a mixture of cigarette ashes and water. Of course we kept these carefully hidden from the Vietnamese.

One of the men received a package from home. He shared everything he had with the rest of us. What a wonderful treat! Actual goodies from home!

Again we received a "gift from the priest."

I shall never forget that Christmas Eve. A group of men quietly singing such carols as "Hark, the Herald Angels Sing" and "Silent Night."

Before retiring, Jim Hivner said, "Everybody who believes in Santa Claus, hang a sock on your mosquito net. Remember, those who believe will receive!"

I did not hang up a sock because I needed to wear them to try to keep warm. We each had two thin blankets but I had to use one of mine as a cushion for my bad hip.

In the quiet of the night, as I had done the two previous Christmas Eves, I mentally shopped for, bought, and wrapped gifts for Ruth and Kevin. *How are they? Are they well? Please, God, let them live normal and happy lives, and know that my thoughts are with them. May God bless and keep them, as well as the other members of the great Ballard family.*

When I awakened the next morning, I found a Christmas card inside my net. The other men had one in their stockings. Jim Hivner had made them without any of us knowing about it!

Christmas, 1969

The first ten months of 1969 were the worst for the POWs. An attempt to escape had failed and the Vietnamese had retaliated with extreme brutality.

In late October, however, a marked improvement in our living conditions came about. We did not know the reason, but the death of Ho Chi Minh may have had something to do with it. I believe now that it was the outstanding support of the American people and the pressure they put upon the North Vietnamese government that brought about the changes.

In December we were allowed to write our first letters home. I had about 800 million things to say to Ruth and questions to ask, but of course this was impossible in a six-line letter.

Several of us received packages from home, which we shared. In mine was a set of thermal underwear, for which I was most grateful. One of my cellmates, Jim Sehorn, had given me one of his blankets. Finally, I could at least stay warm during those long, sleepless, miserable nights.

We made Christmas cards for the men in the other buildings. These were "air-mailed" by tying a rock to the paper and throwing them from our courtyard to theirs.

For a Christmas tree, we decorated a small Swiss-type broom with strips of cloth and paper with various designs. Mike McGrath was quite a good artist and enjoyed doing things with his hands. He used one of his black pajama tops as a background and drew a tree on it. From paper and cloth he made stars and other ornaments and attached them to the tree. Small packages with each of our names were also attached. This was kept hidden during the day but was hung on the wall in the evenings for our enjoyment.

We exchanged gifts that Christmas, both real and imaginary. I gave away gift certificates and treated everyone to a dinner at the Fireside Inn in Las Vegas. One man, who had lost most of his hair, was given a wooden comb. I was given earplugs and a nose clip so I would not be disturbed at night by nearby neighbors!

Christmas Eve the guards came around and gave us the "gift from the priest," also cookies and cigarettes. We were in a good mood as we talked and quietly sang carols until fairly late. Before retiring we each tied a stocking to our nets. I had saved some peanut butter candy from the package Ruth had sent and planned to put some in each man's stocking while they were asleep. I lay awake for about an hour and was just about ready to get up when I heard a noise and looked up. A POW was putting something in my stocking.

He moved quickly from net to net and then sneaked back under his own. Ten minutes later another man got up and did the same thing. It took almost two hours for all eight of us to play Santa Claus.

Early Christmas morning I was awakened by a loud shout from Jim Sehorn: "Merry Christmas, everybody! Get up! He did it! Santa Claus came! Get up! Get up!" What a sight—Jim running from net to net pulling everybody out of bed. Our stockings were full of candy, gifts, and greeting cards.

Later that day the guards came in and removed Mike's shirt with the decorations on it.

He was taken to quiz and the officers told him they were impressed with his art and were going to take it to the museum. Mike told them, "No, you are not." He jerked it off the table and tore it up!

Christmas 1970

In November 1970, there was an unsuccessful attempt by the United States to rescue some POWs from a camp at Son Tay. Within the next few days all of the POWs were moved to downtown Hanoi to a large complex of jails named Hoalo Prison. We called it the Hanoi Hilton. Finally, after so many years, we were all in the same camp, with twenty-five to fifty-six men per cell. We became better organized militarily, academically, and religiously.

That Christmas season was a fairly good one for us. Many men had received packages from home and were allowed to keep the items in their cells. However, a few days before Christmas, the guards removed everything from the cells except for what they had given us.

In October I had received my first letter from home, after more than four years as a prisoner. Included in the letter was a picture of Ruth and Kevin. I prized that picture more than anything in the world and I cannot describe my feelings when the guard took it away.

We began again to scrounge materials for academic purposes, etc. We drew names for gifts. Jim Sehorn gave me a wand and a pendulum to use with my course in hypnotism. I gave him the use of my services for a whole week to hold his legs while he did sit-ups and other exercises.

Christmas Eve the men put on an outstanding play. It was the POW version of Charles Dickens' *Christmas Carol*. Scrooge was played by Dave Ford with Jerry Venanzi directing.

I thoroughly enjoyed the Christmas carols sung by a fifteen-man choir. The singing was disrupted once when a Vietnamese attempted to take pictures through the barred windows. Again we received a "gift from the priest."

That night was a sad one for me. I was reminiscing over past Christmases when I had a strong feeling that my mother had died. (She passed away in August 1969, but I was not notified until our release.)

Christmas morning I was again awakened by Jim Sehorn—with the same enthusiasm and excitement. About this time a most fascinating event occurred—big Tom McNish (six feet, two inches tall) was running up and down the long room with a large bag slung over his shoulder. Tom was dressed in white long-handled underwear and continued his prancing until everyone was up. Then he set down his bag, opened it, and out jumped Santa

Claus! Rod Knutson had on a red suit, black "boots," stocking cap, and a white beard and mustache! I never found out where or how they scrounged all that material. Rod then proceeded to give out hilariously funny imaginary gifts to everyone. We had an exceptionally good meal Christmas Day, and everyone was becoming optimistic about going home soon.

Christmas 1971

Our optimism suffered a setback in early 1971 due to the torturing of many individuals and especially the senior ranking officers. This was in retaliation for our attempts to conduct religious services and to gain improvements in living conditions. The United States had resumed the bombing of North Vietnam. Ten of us had been removed to another large cell along with thirty-four other POWs, all considered to be "diehards" or troublemakers by the Vietnamese.

Christmas, 1971, was about the same as the year before. The choir sang carols, which I thoroughly enjoyed. Six of us non-singers put on a skit imitating the choir. Ed Davis sang a lovely song, one I had never heard before, having to do with Mary and her unborn child, Jesus. I'll never forget Gobel James and his beautiful rendition of "O Holy Night." One man entertained us with his version of *How the Grinch Stole Christmas*.

Tom McNish and Rod Knutson did their Santa Claus number again. Rod gave me some silver oak leaves indicating my promotion to lieutenant colonel. Ruth had written me that it was autumn in Carolina and the silver oak leaves were falling!

Dwight Sullivan presented me with a small poker table, which he had made from bread and sticks. It even had ashtrays. I kept the table for almost a year until the guards finally found it and took it away. I gave my friend Leroy Stutz an imaginary book, *How to Play Winning Poker*, and allowed him to "pin" me at his discretion once per week for a whole month.

Christmas 1972

The bombing of North Vietnam continued into 1972, and many targets near our camp were being attacked. In May over 200 of us were moved to a camp within a few miles of China, in mountainous terrain. Our food and living conditions greatly improved. We were permitted more time outside and given canned meat and various types of vegetable soup to eat with the ever-present rice. Periodically the Vietnamese would go to a nearby village, kill a buffalo, and cook it for us. We conducted weekly bridge and chess tournaments.

I spent one week in solitary confinement due to a minor disagreement with the Vietnamese officers. During this time, my thoughts were mostly with my wife and son. Kevin was now thirteen years old, graduating from high school soon. Hard to believe. I had missed so much of his growing up. One of these days, he would come to me and ask for an automobile.

Most of us were given letters and packages from home that Christmas. There was a picture of Ruth and Kevin on a motorcycle. A black dog lay nearby. I could imagine the companionship that the dog provided for Kevin. I mentally composed a letter to "Blackie." I was both thankful for him and envious of him. He knew more about my son than I did—his habits, stomping grounds, and hiding places.

One of the men heard from the guards that the United States was bombing targets in Hanoi with big bombers night and day. We were jubilant at this news and felt that the attacks would continue until the Vietnamese agreed to release all prisoners.

Christmas Eve, 1972, was a quiet one for us. The choir sang some carols, and that was about it. Our thoughts and prayers were about the future.

In January 1973, we were taken back to the "Hanoi Hilton" and were told that the war was over and we would all be going home soon. What would it be like? How had things changed after six and one-half years of isolation from the real world?

I was among the group of prisoners who was released on March 4, 1973. I did not look back at the camp. I said a prayer that went something like this:

Dear God,

We thank you for taking care of us for such a long time. We now ask that you give us the courage to face the future and to accept the changes that have taken place.

RELIGION IN THE POW CAMPS

In late November of 1970, the United States attempted to rescue some POWs at a camp near Son Tay, North Vietnam. The raid was unsuccessful because the men had been moved to another camp a couple of months earlier.

Within two days all the American prisoners from about five different camps were moved to the "Hanoi Hilton" in downtown Hanoi. The camp consisted of nine cells surrounding a huge courtyard. Each cell consisted of twenty-four to fifty-six men.

We had been denied our request to hold church services, so early in January, probably New Year's Day, Cell 7, consisting of our most senior officers and some others, began singing, very loudly, patriotic songs such as our national anthem and "God Bless America." Soon we in Cell 6 joined them and then Cell 5, etc. We were loud! I am sure everyone in Hanoi heard us.

After twenty minutes of this, some guards came into our cell and removed the senior ranking officer. As he was leaving, the next ranking officer called us to attention and we recited the Lord's Prayer. This infuriated the guards and they took him also. As he was leaving, the next SRO called us to attention and we again recited the Lord's Prayer. They eventually removed four or five of our SROs from our cell. The same type of thing was happening in all the cells. All told, twenty-five to thirty of our seniors were removed, placed in solitary confinement in leg irons and wrist cuffs, and on short rations for approximately three months.

In the meantime the Vietnamese relented somewhat and allowed us to conduct fifteen-minute services with no more than a five-man choir. They would station two armed guards in our cells, one at each end, during the services.

Eventually the guards got tired of this and would not come into the cells. We gradually escalated the service into a somewhat normal Protestant type.

QUESTIONS I HAVE BEEN ASKED

1. How did you learn you were finally going home?

    When the bombing increased so dramatically in December 1972, we felt that this time the United States would keep it up until the Vietnamese agreed to release all the prisoners. And that is what happened. At the end of a two-week period, our aircraft were flying unmolested all over North Vietnam. Our bombers had destroyed their military.

    One of the conditions agreed to in January was to give each POW a copy of the agreement. At the time, about two hundred of us were living in a camp near China. We were not told of the signing until we returned to the Hanoi Hilton complex later that month. We were given a copy and found out that we would be going home in the order of shoot-down date. (The ones shot down the earliest would go home first.) The first group of about 100 POWs was released on February 12. I was in the second large group released on March 4, 1973. A happy day.

2. What were some of the problems you experienced upon returning home?

    Our first stop was in the Philippine Islands at Clark Air Force Base. When I called Ruth, I knew immediately that everything was going to be all right. She sounded so strong and confident. What a beautiful voice.

Of course, there were many problems. I had to get used to my family, and they to me. Kevin was six years old when I left home and now he was thirteen with long hair; when I first saw him, I thought he was one of the escort officers for Ruth. He and I slowly got to know each other and accepted our differences. Kevin is, and I say this gratefully, not boastfully, a high IQ person. He has completed an MD, PhD and is currently Director of Research and Development with NMS Labs in Pennsylvania.

I think the hardest things for me to accept were the tremendous changes in society. Moral standards had deteriorated so much. Co-habitation of students in college. Drug use. I was disappointed in the leaders in academia and our government.

It took a long time to regain my health. I was hospitalized several times for surgery and various illnesses. I had to have part of my skull removed and replaced with acrylic plastic. I probably had been kicked in the head during one of the torture sessions, which had caused the damage. Because of the surgery, I was grounded from flying.

Large, noisy crowds disturbed me to a great extent, and still do. When the POWs came home, we were treated as heroes. Everywhere I went there were people, a great many of them strangers; yet they wanted to be near me or touch me. Whenever a POW was in a crowd in Vietnam, the crowd was hostile. Convincing myself that the crowds are friendly has been an ongoing process.

At first driving was unnerving. I recall feeling that things were moving too swiftly. At that moment, I would pull over and ask Ruth to drive.

Long periods of concentration were difficult. Some of this is undoubtedly due to years of malnutrition, plus relearning how to study. I attended Air War College during the day and Troy State University in the evening, where I received an undergraduate and a master's degree.

There have been nightmares and occasional "flashbacks" but these occur less frequently now.

3. Do you keep in touch with any POWs from your camp?

    We have an organization called "Fourth Allied POW Wing." We elect officers and one of their functions is to put out a newsletter periodically. Contributions are sent in by the former POWs, so we pretty much keep up with each other. Once in a while a friend will call (usually at 3:00 AM!) just wanting to talk. I got a call late one afternoon from a former cellmate who had landed at the downtown Spartanburg airport. He was on his way to Florida to visit his mother. He has his own airplane. I picked him up and brought him home to have dinner with us. He stayed a week!

4. Other than seeing your family and friends, what was the first thing you wanted to do when you returned?

    Eat a good breakfast! As I recall, I wanted to see and do everything. I wanted to reacquaint myself with this wonderful land of freedom. I wanted to go to a baseball game. The Spartanburg Phillies honored me at opening season 1973 by asking me to throw out the first ball.

I also wanted to go to a supermarket; something that I avoided like the plague before Vietnam. I still remember my reaction the first time Ruth and I went grocery shopping. Seeing all the shelves and cases filled with tantalizing food items caused an unpredictable impulse: I had to fight the urge to grab armfuls and run with them! It had been seven years since I had seen food displayed in a plentiful manner.

5. Looking in hindsight, was there anything you would have done differently as a prisoner of war?

I cannot think of anything that I would have done differently. Decisions have to be made according to existing circumstances. I am sure I would have changed some things if I had had no injuries, such as planning for and possibly attempting an escape.

6. Because of your experience, how do you look at life differently than you did before your plane was shot down?

Little things no longer bother me. Life is too precious and fleeting to be bogged down in triviality.

7. Why do you believe the US became involved in Vietnam?

At the time, the national policy of the US was to contain communism. I felt, and so did most military people, that we were involved in accomplishing that mission. We had been doing that since the end of World War II, in Korea, Cuba, and several other places. I hated to see one country trying to take over another. I felt strongly that people should have the freedom to make up their own minds as to what type of government they want.

8. Was there a particular reason you stopped writing your manuscript (when) you were transferred to Camp Faith?

The death of Ho Chi Minh and our subsequent move to Camp Faith marked a change in the lives of the POWs. The mass torturing was stopped. There was still some torturing to get individuals or small groups to make propaganda statements or talk to visitors from various countries. There was more or less a live-and-let-live atmosphere as long we obeyed the camp regulations. We began living in large groups—anywhere from twenty-five to fifty POWs in each cell.

But looking back to when I wrote the manuscript, I don't think I stopped because it marked a change in our treatment. It had taken several years to write the small amount that I did. When I was thinking of what to write, of necessity I had to remember even the smallest details. That would get to me after a time; then I would stop writing and come back to it some months later. Perhaps I will finish the story someday.

9. Do you believe that there are still POWs and MIAs in Vietnam?

When we were released in early 1973, I did not think that we left anyone there. I did not think that the Vietnamese had any reason to keep any of us. We had lived in several different camps and we felt that we knew the names of all who had been captured and their status. Some had died in camp, but all POWs we knew were accounted for at the time of our release.

It seems from recently gathered information that many who had been captured in Laos were not released. I doubt seriously that any of them have survived. It would be nice to know that some of my friends were still alive, but what shape would they be in after all these years?

However, I do think we should find out for sure where the missing are, and bring them home for a proper burial. If they are alive, take an army over there and bring them home.

ANSWERS TO DEVIN'S QUESTIONS (EIGHTH GRADE NEPHEW)

1. Why did we join the Vietnam War?

A lot of things happened at the end of World War II. The Soviet Union had already formed a Communist government and begun militarily taking over European countries—Czechoslovakia, Romania, and Poland. At that time President Truman decided not to allow the USSR to expand any further. He gave military and economic aid to Greece and Turkey to help prevent them from being taken over by the Soviet Union. Thus, the United States' "Policy of Containment" became official.

This containment policy got us into the Korean War in the early 1950s, when communist North Korea attempted to conquer South Korea. Eventually we pushed them out of South Korea and established a demarcation zone between the two countries. That is how it stands today. Technically we are still at war with them; a cease-fire still exists. We maintain a strong military presence in South Korea to guarantee their freedom.

Pretty much the same thing got us involved in the Vietnam War. After World War II the French regained control of all Vietnam. A fellow named Ho Chi Minh left Vietnam, went to Russia, and studied communism. He returned to Vietnam, formed an army, and defeated the French. He then established a communist government in North Vietnam and wanted to unite all of Vietnam under communism. Finally an agreement was reached whereby an election would be held to determine what kind of government the country would be under. I think Ho Chi Minh and the USSR felt that the people would vote for a Democratic type of government, so they refused to hold elections. They began to try to take over South Vietnam by military force.

Our involvement was gradual: at first just sending advisors, then later sending our own troops. This was in keeping with our policy of containing the expansion of communism.

2. Should civil wars be fought between that country?

That's a tough question and it has been hotly debated over the years. I do not think that the war in Southeast Asia was a civil war because of the way it evolved. We went over there to prevent one country from taking over another by force. I do not like communism. I have seen how it works and how it affects people. People live miserably under those conditions. I guess what makes me different from a lot of other people is that I care about others. Freedom is one thing I value so highly and I hate to see anyone deprived of that freedom. Read the Bill of Rights. I enjoy being able to vote for whom I wish; to travel wherever I wish; to say or write whatever I wish. People living under communism do not have those rights.

3. As a Christian how did you feel about killing the enemy and possibly innocent people?

Nobody likes to go to war. It is a last resort after all else fails. It is a terrible thing. But it is not as terrible as living under a dictatorship, which is really what communism is all about. So when the decision is finally made to go to war, killing is an unavoidable necessity. Our objective in Vietnam was to prevent the flow of supplies from North Vietnam to their forces in the south. We did this by destroying railroads, roads, bridges, oil storage areas, trains, trucks, and enemy troops. If we did not do this, then many more US soldiers would be killed or severely wounded. We did not intentionally kill innocent civilians. But I know that it does happen accidentally sometimes. Many times I saw big guns shooting at us from the middle of a village or downtown Hanoi. We did not attack these guns because even a near miss would jeopardize civilians. I know from post-mission reports that I killed many soldiers. I did not enjoy the killing. But that is what war is all about.

4. Let's say you lived during the time of the Civil War and you volunteered or were drafted: Which side would you have been on? Why?

When I was growing up around the mill villages of Spartanburg, there was a feeling of strong support for family, friends, and the community. We were completely loyal to each other and would have fought to protect each other.

I am sure I would have had those same feelings during the time of the Civil War and would have fought for the South. (However), had I been over thirty years old during that time, it might have been different. I would have considered the causes of the war—economic conditions, the right to secede from the Union, the election of Abraham Lincoln, slavery—and might very well have sided with the North.

AIR REFUELING

Dick Lougee and I were first lieutenants and had been flying the F-100C for a little more than a year with the 436th Fighter Day Squadron at George Air Force Base, California. We were given the task of learning how to air refuel with a modified version of the B-29, a World War II bomber. It was re-designated the KB-50.

The "Probe and Drogue" method consisted of a ten-foot-long probe attached to the right wing of the F-100 and a fifty-foot-long hose with a basket on the end trailing from the KB-50.

The probe could not be seen from the cockpit, so our job was to figure out what reference on the tanker to use as a guideline to line up with the basket, what closing speed to use, and how to make a successful hookup.

Dick outranked me by a few months, so he was the first to try. After several attempts I could tell he was getting frustrated. Finally he said, "#$@^&## it, Ted! You try it!"

As I approached the basket I could see that the air disturbed by my aircraft would push the basket up, down, or sideways. Once I overshot and the basket and hose were bouncing on my canopy! Another time I thought I was connected, but the guy in the KB-50 told me I was hooked up with my drop tank!

I was finally successful after about a dozen attempts, and then Dick tried again and got the hang of it. Some months later the probe was lengthened and curved upward so the pilot could see it and just guide it into the basket.

A couple of years later we began flying the new F-104, which had a refueling arm on the left side of the front fuselage, so refueling was much easier. The KB-50 was remodeled by adding four jet engines so we could maintain a higher speed for refueling.

When I began flying the F-105, air refueling was a piece o' cake, because now we were using the KC-135, which had a boom extended from its rear and had an airman sitting there guiding it. All we had to do was position ourselves behind the KC-135, open a refueling door in the top of the fuselage, and the airman would give us fuel. The F-105 also had an "arm" which could be extended from the fuselage in case we needed to use the basket method.

During the war in Vietnam we had to use the KC-135 on almost every mission, both en route to and returning from the target. The KC-135 would orbit either over Laos or the South China Sea to await our return. Several times when we used too much fuel in the target area due to MiGs or too much afterburner, we would call the tanker, and he would immediately fly into North Vietnam to meet us so we could get enough fuel to get back home. Without the tankers' bravery, many of us would not have made it.

TURK TURLEY

Mike, Turk, Ted

Two weeks prior to my shoot-down I was given the task of filling out the schedule: assigning flights to particular targets and takeoff times. This had been Major Turk Turley's job, but he was in the process of taking over as operations officer, second in command of the squadron. Major Ron Johnson was near 100 missions, the maximum number of flights for a tour, and would be going back to the States soon.

I was the flight commander of "D" Flight, and Turk flew most of his missions with us. I asked him one night why he scheduled himself to fly on the tough missions in and around Hanoi. He said, "Ted, I feel obligated. We've already lost ten aircraft and four pilots and I just have to be there."

Mike Thomas was my assistant flight commander. On September 26, 1966, our target was an oil storage area north of Hanoi. Turk asked me to let him lead that mission, so he became "Pinto" lead; Captain Don Quigley #2; Captain Mike Thomas #3; and I was #4. First Lt. Chuck Haberstich was the spare pilot, who would start up with us and wait awhile to fill in if someone had to abort.

We had all flown together many times except for Don Quigley. He had just arrived a couple of weeks before and I had checked him out on a few flights. This was my 68th mission. We were to take off about one hour before sunrise. After startup Turk radioed that he had maintenance problems and would abort. As we had briefed, Mike became lead, I moved up to number three, and Chuck became number four. Takeoff was normal except my airspeed indicator became inoperative. I did not say anything because I wasn't going to let them go without me. I could fly somebody's wing when we came back for landing.

We rendezvoused with the KC-135 tanker over Laos, took on a full load of fuel, then headed north across the Black River and then the Red River. I had been somewhat nervous up until that point. (I was nervous for a while on some missions, others not so much but always alert.) When we headed east after crossing the Red, I was too busy to worry about anything except for navigating, checking for enemy aircraft, and keeping everybody in sight. A flight five minutes ahead of us was dodging missiles. As we approached that area we descended to a lower altitude to make it tougher for radar to track us. We were just beginning to climb back up slightly when my aircraft was hit, probably by 57-mm guns. I had not seen any 85- or 100-mm yet. My capture and internment are documented in my memoir, *From the Dungeons of North Vietnam*.

In October 2007, the three fighter squadrons that had been stationed at Okinawa had their first reunion. It was just great to see my friends again. At one of the events Turk took me aside and said he wanted to tell me something that had been on his mind for a long time. He said that my shoot-down had affected the whole squadron, more than any of the others. When Mike, Chuck, and Don returned from the mission they went directly to the squadron commander, Lt. Col. Dick Baughn, and said they did not want to fly any more missions. I think they were frustrated because we weren't allowed to bomb certain targets such as the airfields and Haiphong Harbor, where supplies were being shipped in from Russia. Col. Baughn asked Turk to counsel them.

Mike was worried that he had done something wrong that caused my aircraft to be shot down. They discussed the route and Turk told him that he had flown it exactly as he would have. Even so they were emphatic that they weren't going to fly any more missions. Turk told them they were on the schedule for tomorrow, but if they were sincere, to pack their bags, take an R&R to Bangkok, and nothing would be said. If they were not present for duty, he would find other pilots to take their place. He advised them to think about what Ted would want them to do. The next day they were present and ready to fly again.

I was the last one of the original 13th Squadron members to be shot down. Most completed 100 missions and had successful careers in the Air Force. Dick Baughn became a general. My roommate, Will

Snell, who had already completed 100 and gone home, eventually made full colonel. Bob Hannah and Mike Thomas retired as lieutenant colonels. I saw Chuck Haberstich when I was released and he was a major at that time. No one has heard from him since. John Thigpen was killed in an aircraft accident in the States later.

I got in touch with most of them several years ago, and we email often. Last August I received an email from Turk, which said simply that he had a temperature of 102 and was on his way to the hospital.

The next day, another squadron member, Tom Lockhart, sent the following message:

> "It is with great sadness that I report that Turk Turley has gone 'West.' Nancy just called and there are no funeral arrangements yet. Details to follow. Regrets, Tom Lockhart"

Later I learned that the doctor said the cause was probably pneumonia. Turk's body was cremated and services were held in California and later at Arlington. I was unable to attend either service due to back problems.

Tom gave the eulogy at Turk's funeral and this is part of what he said:

> "I have described my mentor, my friend, and my hero to you as best I can. I would like, now, to read this poem which has no name and whose author is unknown. For today, I would call it:

FROM THE DUNGEONS OF NORTH VIETNAM

A Warrior's Farewell

When I come to the end of the day,
and the sun has set for me,
I want no rites in a gloom-filled room.
Why cry for a soul set free.

Miss me but let me go...

Miss me a little, but not too long
and not with your head bowed low.
Remember the love we once shared.

Miss me but let me go...

For this is a journey we all must take
and each must travel alone.
It's all a part of the Maker's plan
a step on the road to home.

Miss me but let me go...

When you are lonely and sick at heart,
go to the friends we know,
bury your sorrows in doing good deeds.

Miss me but let me go."

"You will be missed, my friend. You will be missed. And so watch
well, ye Valkyries, warriors of Valhalla! Watch for the mighty Turk...
and proudly escort him into your hallowed hall. Valhalla...where
fallen warriors are chosen... Where the brave, they live forever."

ROSCOE

Not long after I arrived at Korat Air Base in Thailand, I became aware of a reddish brown dog that lived on base, near or under our "hootch." He took to the men in our squadron right away. Roscoe seemed to sense that we came from the same base on Okinawa that he did. A pilot from Kadena Air Base had brought Roscoe with him the year before. The pilot was shot down over North Vietnam and was listed as missing in action.

Roscoe became everybody's dog, and was the only dog allowed on base. He would greet each flight that returned from a mission, looking for his master. He attended most of the briefings that preceded all missions, especially the ones that required a large number of airplanes. Roscoe seemed to possess a sixth sense. He would sit in the seat next to the wing commander. If his ears perked up and he seemed restless, we knew it would be a tough mission. On the other hand, if he fell asleep, we would relax ourselves, knowing it would be a fairly uneventful flight.

I was one of four flight commanders, each with six pilots. Each flight had a small pickup truck to drive to and from the flight line and to run various errands. Roscoe would ride with us when we left the hootch and went to the Officer's Club for breakfast. We would feed him whatever we had to eat. Then he would continue to ride with us to the flight line for the briefing for that day's target. When we returned from the mission and had been debriefed, he would join us for the ride back to the Club for lunch. Sometimes he wasn't hungry and would not get out of the truck at the Club. He would look at me and I could see that he wanted to go back to the hootch—so I would drive him home and then return to the Club. I remember Roscoe riding with us on the day that I was shot down. He ate breakfast with us and attended the briefing but I cannot recall his reactions.

A few years after the war a group of pilots from my old squadron visited Korat Air Base and found a gravestone just outside the old Officer's Club. Engraved on the stone was one word: "ROSCOE."

The men of the 44th Tactical Fighter Squadron donated a plaque to tell his story:

HERE LIES ROSCOE
CAME TO KORAT IN 1965 DIED HERE ON
13 SEPT 1975

"I SPENT ALL OF MY LIFE WAITING FOR MY MASTER,
BUT HE NEVER RETURNED FROM NORTH VIETNAM.
NOW WE ARE TOGETHER,
AND I AM HAPPY TO SEE HIM AGAIN.
ONLY GOD CAN PART US NOW."

A few years ago, some retired fighter pilots and their wives visited the burial site and found it fitting, set aside by the Thais and kept in excellent condition. One of the ladies said, "All of a sudden you're standing in a crowd, but you are not." The Thais had an expression that meant, "It is a place of many strong spirits."

I can visualize that place and remember old friends, many of whom are no longer with us.

PART THREE

Lt. Col. A.T. Ballard, Jr.
North Vietnam
26 September 1966 - 4 March 1973

4th ALLIED P.O.W. WING

4

RETURN WITH HONOR

RETURN WITH HONOR

MAXWELL
AIR FORCE BASE, ALABAMA
Decorations Ceremony

1973

These six former POWs of the Southeast Asia War were honored recently in an awards ceremony held by Lt. Gen. F. Michael Rogers, Air University Commander. The six are: Front Row (left to right): Col Arnand J. Myers, Lt. Col. Arthur T. Ballard, and Lt. Col. John J. Pitchford. Back Roe (left to right): Col. Carlyle S. Harris, Lt. Col. Robert B. Parcell, and Lt. Col. William H. Means, Jr.

(USAF Photo by SSgt Bennie Sanders)
Article from "The Dispatch", Dispatch Publishers

Veteran Tributes
Honoring Those Who Served

Arthur T. Ballard, Jr.

Lieutenant Colonel 0-5, U.S. Air Force

Veteran Of:

U.S.A.F. - 1954 - 1975

Cold War 1954 - 1975

Vietnam War - 1965 - 1973

Ted Ballard was born in 1932 in Spartanburg, South Carolina. He enlisted in the Aviation Cadet Program of the U.S. Air Force on January 15, 1954, and was commissioned a 2d Lt and awarded his pilot wings at Greenville AFB, Mississippi, on June 1, 1955. After completing gunnery training in the T-33 Shooting Star and F-86 Sabre Combat Crew Training, Ballard was assigned to the 436th and then the 476th Tactical Fighter Squadron at George AFB, California, where he flew the F-100A & C Super Sabre and the F-104C Starfighter from January 1956 to March 1960. His next assignment was flying F-100's with the 7272nd Air Base Wing at Wheelus AB, Libya, from March 1960 to March 1963. Capt Ballard then served as a Command Post Controller with the 4520th Combat Crew Training Wing, followed by F-105 Thunderchief Combat Crew Training, at Nellis AFB, Nevada, from April 1963 to August 1965. Ballard then flew F-105's with the 44th Tactical Fighter Squadron at Kadena AB, Okinawa, from September 1965 to June 1966. He flew 68 combat missions with the 13th Tactical Fighter Squadron at Korat Royal Thai AFB, Thailand, from June 1966 until he was forced to eject over North Vietnam on September 26, 1966. After spending 2,351 days in captivity, Col Ballard was released during Operation Homecoming on March 4, 1973. He was briefly hospitalized to recover from his injuries at Andrews AFB, Maryland, and then attended Air War College at Maxwell AFB, Alabama, from August 1973 to August 1974. Col Ballard remained on the faculty of the Air War College until his retirement from the Air Force on July 31, 1975. After his retirement from the Air Force, Ted taught Air Force Junior ROTC at Gaffney High School in Gaffney, South Carolina, for 22 years. He and his wife, Ruth, had one child, Kevin Dale Ballard, (27 Oct. 1959 – 6 May 2009) His Silver Star Citation reads:

This officer distinguished himself by gallantry and intrepidity in action in connection with military operations against an opposing armed force while a Prisoner of War in North Vietnam. Ignoring international agreements on treatment of prisoners of war, the enemy resorted to mental and physical cruelties to obtain information, confessions, and propaganda materials. This American resisted their demands by calling upon his deepest inner strengths in a manner which reflected his devotion to duty and great credit upon himself and the United States Air Force.

Lieutenant Colonel

Arthur Theodore Ballard, Jr.

Air Force

Awarded for actions during the Vietnam War

Lt. Col. Ballard was interned as a Prisoner of War in North Vietnam,

From September 26, 1966, until his release on March 4, 1973.

SILVER STAR

Action Date: 10-Oct-66

Citation:

The President of the United States of America, authorized by Act of Congress, July 8, 1918 (amended by act of July 25, 1963), takes pleasure in presenting the Silver Star to Lieutenant Colonel Arthur Theodore Ballard, Jr. (AFSN: OF-31816), United States Air Force, for gallantry and intrepidity in action in connection with military operations against an opposing armed force on 10 October 1966, while a Prisoner of War in North Vietnam. Ignoring international agreements on treatment of prisoners of war, the enemy resorted to mental and physical cruelties to obtain information, confessions, and propaganda materials. Lieutenant Colonel Ballard resisted their demands by calling upon his deepest inner strengths in a manner, which reflected his devotion to duty, and great credit upon himself and the United States Air Force.

The Silver Star is the third-highest military combat decoration that can be awarded to a member of the United States Armed Forces. Actions that merit the Silver Star must be of such a high degree that they are above those required for all other U.S. combat decorations, with the exceptions of the Medal of Honor or a Service Cross. It is awarded for gallantry in action:

★ While engaged in action against an enemy of the United States;

★ While engaged in military operations involving conflict with an opposing foreign force; or

★ While serving with friendly foreign forces engaged in an armed conflict against an opposing armed force in which the United States is not a belligerent party.

Lieutenant Colonel

Arthur Theodore Ballard, Jr.

Air Force

Awarded for actions during the Vietnam War

Lt. Col. Ballard was interned as a Prisoner of War in North Vietnam,

From September 26, 1966, until his release on March 4, 1973.

LEGION OF MERIT

Action Date: September 1966 - November 1970

Citation:

The President of the United States of America, authorized by Act of Congress, 20 July 1942, takes pleasure in presenting the Legion of Merit to Lieutenant Colonel Arthur Theodore Ballard, Jr. (AFSN: OF-31816), United States Air Force, for exceptionally meritorious conduct in the performance of outstanding services to the Government of the United States as a Prisoner of War in North Vietnam from September 1966 - November 1970. His ceaseless efforts, by a continuous showing of resistance to an enemy who ignored all International agreements on treatment of Prisoners of War, in the extremely adverse conditions of the communist prisons of North Vietnam, demonstrated his professional competence, unwavering devotion, and loyalty to his country. Despite the harsh treatment through his long years of incarceration, he continued to perform his duties in a clearly exceptional manner, which reflected great credit upon himself and the United States Air Force.

The Legion of Merit (LOM) is a military award of the United States Armed Forces that is given for exceptionally meritorious conduct in the performance of outstanding services and achievements. The decoration is issued both to United States military personnel and to military and political figures of foreign governments.

The Legion of Merit (Commander degree) is one of only two United States military decorations to be issued as a neck order (the other being the Medal of Honor) and the only United States decoration which may be issued in award degrees (much like an order of chivalry or certain Orders of Merit).

The Legion of Merit is sixth in the order of precedence of U.S. Military awards and is worn after the Defense Superior Service Medal and before the Distinguished Flying Cross. In contemporary use in the U.S. Armed Forces, the Legion of Merit is typically awarded to Army, Marine Corps, and Air Force General Officers and Colonels, and Navy and Coast Guard Flag Officers and Captains occupying command or very senior staff positions in their respective services.

Arthur Theodore Ballard, Jr.

Service: Air Force

Division: Prisoner of War (North Vietnam)

Rank: Lieutenant Colonel

Bronze Star Medal

(With "V" Device)

(First Oak Leaf Cluster)

AWARDED FOR ACTIONS DURING THE VIETNAM WAR

ACTION DATE: JANUARY 1971 TO MARCH 1972

Citation:

This officer distinguished himself by heroic achievement as a Prisoner of War while engaged in operations against an opposing armed force in North Vietnam during the above period. In an atmosphere of enemy harassment and brutal treatment, he continued to establish and maintain communications through unusual and ingenious methods, which resulted in America and Allied prisoners presenting a posture of increased resistance to the enemy's wishes, and, at the same time, improving prisoner morale. By his heroic endeavors and devotion to duty under adverse conditions of his environment, he reflected great credit upon himself and the United States Air Force.

When awarded for acts of heroism, the Bronze Star is award with the "V" device. This medal is the United States Military's fourth highest decoration for valor. In the Army and the Air Force, the device denotes that a specific individual decoration resulted from an act of combat heroism.

Lieutenant Colonel

Arthur Theodore Ballard, Jr.

Air Force

Awarded for actions during the Vietnam War

Lt. Col. Ballard was interned as a Prisoner of War in North Vietnam,

From September 26, 1966, until his release on March 4, 1973.

Bronze Star Medal

AWARDED FOR ACTIONS DURING THE VIETNAM WAR

ACTION DATE: 13 May 1966- 26 September 1966

Citation:

Captain Arthur T. Ballard, Jr., distinguished himself by meritorious service as a Flight Commander and Scheduling Office for the 13th Tactical Fighter Squadron, Korat Royal Thai Air Force Base, Thailand, from 13 May 1966 to 26 September 1966. In these important assignments, the leadership, tactical knowledge, and ceaseless efforts consistently demonstrated by Captain Ballard resulted in significant contributions to the effectiveness and success of tactical airpower in the furtherance of the United States National Policies in Southeast Asia. Captain Ballard's rigid personal discipline, influence upon crew reliability, technical knowledge, and potential have contributed significantly to the sustained F-105 mission capability. The exemplary leadership, personal endeavor, and devotion to duty displayed by Captain Ballard in these responsibilities reflect great credit upon himself and the United States Air Force.

PART THREE: RETURN WITH HONOR

The Bronze Star Medal is awarded to any person who, while serving in any way in or with the United States military after 6 December 1941, distinguished himself or herself apart from his or her comrades by brave or praiseworthy achievement or service. The act justifying award of the medal must be performed while fighting an enemy of the United States, or while involved in conflict with an opposing/foreign force. It can also be awarded for heroism while serving with friendly forces engaged in combat against an opposing military in which the United States is not a belligerent party. Heroism carried out under acts as described, which are of a lesser degree than those awarded of the *Silver Star*, will justify the award of the Bronze Star Medal. While of a lesser degree than the award of the *Legion of Merit*, the act justifying the awarding of the Bronze Star Medal must have been praiseworthy and accomplished with merit. It can be awarded for a single act of value or meritorious service.

Lieutenant Colonel

Arthur Theodore Ballard, Jr.

Air Force

Awarded for actions during the Vietnam War

Lt. Col. Ballard was interned as a Prisoner of War in North Vietnam,

From September 26, 1966, until his release on March 4, 1973.

Distinguished Flying Cross (2 Awards)

*AWARDED FOR ACTIONS DURING THE **VIETNAM WAR***

ACTION DATE: 22 August 1966

Citation:

Captain Arthur T. Ballard, Jr. distinguished himself by heroism while participating in aerial flight as an F-105 Pilot over North Vietnam on 22 August 1966. On that date, Captain Ballard flew his heavily laden Thunderchief, armed with high explosives against a strategic petroleum area located 10 miles northwest of Hanoi, North Vietnam. Although the target area was engulfed in flak, he elected to continue his bomb run. Pulling off the target, he was attacked by hostile aircraft. His F105 was damaged, but he was able to return safely to his home base. The outstanding heroism and selfless devotion to duty displayed by Captain Ballard reflect great credit upon himself and the United States Air Force.

The Distinguished Flying Cross, created by Congress eighty years ago, is America's oldest military aviation award. The cross symbolizes sacrifice, and the propeller symbolizes flight. The combination of those symbols makes clear that the DFC is an award for heroism or achievement for individuals involved in aviation. The ribbon reflects the national colors.

The cross consists of a 1½-inch cross pattée, on which is superimposed a four-bladed propeller projecting slightly beyond the ends of the cross. In the angles of the cross are five sunrays forming a square typifying the glory and splendor of the deed for which the cross is awarded. The medal is suspended from a red, white, and blue ribbon.

Lieutenant Colonel

Arthur Theodore Ballard, Jr.

Air Force

Awarded for actions during the Vietnam War

Lt. Col. Ballard was interned as a Prisoner of War in North Vietnam,

From September 26, 1966, until his release on March 4, 1973.

Distinguished Flying Cross

ACTION DATE: 1 September 1966

Lieutenant Colonel Arthur Theodore Ballard, Jr. (AFSN: OF-31816), United States Air Force, was awarded a Bronze Oak Leaf Cluster in lieu of a Second Award of the Distinguished Flying Cross for extraordinary achievement while participating in aerial flight in Southeast Asia.

Citation:

Captain Arthur T. Ballard, Jr., distinguished himself by heroism while participating in aerial flight as an F-105 Pilot over North Vietnam on 1 September 1966. On that date, Captain Ballard flew his heavily laden Thunderchief armed high explosive bombs against a strategic petroleum storage area located in the heart of North Vietnam industrial complex. Inbound to the target, three surface to air missiles were fired at his flight, and MIGS were encountered in the area. Although intense and accurate flak engulfed his target are, he made his bomb run and scored a direct hit, destroying a vital petroleum area. The outstanding heroism and selfless devotion to duty displayed by Captain Ballard reflect great credit upon himself and the United States Air Force.

Subsequent awards of the Distinguished Flying Cross are indicated by oak-leaf clusters for Army and Air Force personnel.

Lieutenant Colonel

Arthur Theodore Ballard, Jr.

Air Force

Awarded for actions during the Vietnam War

Lt. Col. Ballard was interned as a Prisoner of War in North Vietnam,

From September 26, 1966, until his release on March 4, 1973.

USAF Air Medal (8 Awards)

ACTION DATE: from 4 July 1966 to 26 September 1966

Citation:

Captain Arthur T. Ballard, Jr., distinguished himself by meritorious achievement while participating in sustained aerial flight as an F-105 Pilot in Southeast Asia from 4 July 1966 to 26 September 1966. During this period, outstanding airmanship and courage were exhibited in the successful accomplishment of important missions under extremely hazardous conditions including the continuous possibility of hostile ground fire. His highly professional efforts contributed materially to the mission of the United States Air Force in Southeast Asia. The professional ability and outstanding aerial accomplishments of Captain Ballard reflect great credit upon himself and the United States Air Force.

The Air Medal, established by Executive Order 9158, 11 May 1942, as amended by Executive Order 9242, 11 September 1942 is awarded for single acts of heroism or meritorious achievements to military personnel in actual combat in support of operations. Required achievement is less than that required for the Distinguished Flying Cross, but must be accomplished with distinction above and beyond that expected of professional aviators. It is not awarded for peacetime sustained operational activities and flights.

The medal is a bronze compass rose of sixteen points that is surrounded by a fleur-de-lis design in the top point. On the obverse, in the center, is an American eagle, swooping downward (attacking) and clutching a lightning bolt in each talon. The reverse has a raised disk on the compass rose, left blank for the recipient's name and rank.

The ribbon has a broad stripe of ultramarine blue in the center flanked on either side by a wide stripe of golden orange, and with a narrow stripe of ultramarine blue at the edge—the original colors of the Army Air Corps.

Lieutenant Colonel

Arthur Theodore Ballard, Jr.

Air Force

Awarded for actions during the Vietnam War

Lt. Col. Ballard was interned as a Prisoner of War in North Vietnam,

From September 26, 1966, until his release on March 4, 1973.

Prisoner of War Medal

Awarded for actions during the Vietnam War

Action Date: September 26, 1966 - March 4, 1973

Citation:

Lieutenant Colonel Arthur Theodore Ballard, Jr. (AFSN: OF-31816), United States Air Force, was held as a Prisoner of War in North Vietnam from September 26, 1966 until his release on March 4, 1973.

The Prisoner of War Medal is a military award of the United States Armed Forces which was authorized by Congress and signed into law by President Ronald Reagan on 8 November 1985. The United States Code citation for the POW Medal statute is 10 U.S.C. § 1128. The Prisoner of War Medal may be awarded to any person who was a prisoner after April 5, 1917 (the date of the United States' entry into World War I was April 6). It is awarded to any person who was taken prisoner or held captive while engaged in an action against an enemy of the United States; while engaged in military operations involving conflict with an opposing Armed Force; or while serving with friendly forces engaged in armed conflict against an opposing Armed Force in which the United States is not a belligerent party. As of an amendment to Title 10 of the United States Code in 2013, the medal is also awarded for captivity under circumstances "which the Secretary concerned finds were comparable to those circumstances under which persons have generally been held captive by enemy armed forces during periods of armed conflict." The person's conduct while in captivity must have been honorable.

Lieutenant Colonel

Arthur Theodore Ballard, Jr.

Air Force

Awarded for actions during the Vietnam War

Lt. Col. Ballard was interned as a Prisoner of War in North Vietnam,

From September 26, 1966, until his release on March 4, 1973.

Air Force Commendation Medal

Awarded for actions during the Vietnam War

Citation:

This officer distinguished himself by meritorious achievement in the performance of duties involving highly classified material while detained as a Prisoner of War in North Vietnam during the above period. He performed these duties while under constant surveillance of the enemy and generated new ideas and improvised techniques which greatly enhanced covert operations. His commendable performance and dedication to duty reflected credit upon himself and the United States Air Force.

The Air Force Commendation Medal was authorized by the Secretary of the Air Force on March 28, 1958, for award to members of the Armed Forces of the United States who, while serving in any capacity with the Air Force after March 24, 1958, shall have distinguished themselves by meritorious achievement and service. The degree of merit must be distinctive, though it need not be unique.

Medal Description

The medal is a bronze hexagon, with one point up, centered upon which is the seal of the Air Force, an eagle with wings spread, facing left and perched upon a baton. There are clouds in the background. Below the seal is a shield bearing a pair of flyer's wings and a vertical baton with an eagle's claw at either end; behind the shield are eight lightning bolts.

Lieutenant Colonel

Arthur Theodore Ballard, Jr.

Air Force

Awarded for actions during the Vietnam War

Lt. Col. Ballard was interned as a Prisoner of War in North Vietnam,

From September 26, 1966, until his release on March 4, 1973.

Purple Heart (2)

Action Dates: 26 September 1966

26 September 1966 to 4 March 1973

THE UNITED STATES OF AMERICA

THE PURPLE HEART

The Purple Heart is awarded in the name of the President of the United States to any member of an Armed Force or any civilian national of the United States who, while serving under competent authority in any capacity with one of the U.S. Armed Services after 5 April 1917, has been wounded or killed, or who has died or may hereafter die after being wounded. While clearly an individual decoration, the Purple Heart differs from all other decorations in that an individual is not "recommended" for the decoration; rather he or she is entitled to it upon meeting specific criteria.

(1) A Purple Heart is authorized for the first wound suffered under conditions indicated above, but for each subsequent award, an Oak Leaf Cluster will be awarded to be worn on the medal or ribbon. Not more than one award will be made for more than one wound or injury received at the same instant or from the same missile, force, explosion, or agent.

(2) A wound is defined as an injury to any part of the body from an outside force or agent sustained under one or more of the conditions listed above. A physical lesion is not required; however, the wound for which the award is made must have required treatment by a medical officer, and records of medical treatment for wounds or injuries received in action must have been made a matter of official record.

PART FOUR

TIMELINE

LIFE TIMELINE

Lieutenant Colonel Arthur "Ted" Ballard, Jr. was born 1 February 1932 in Spartanburg, South Carolina, the second child of nine born to Arthur T. and Carrie Ballard. Ted graduated from Spartanburg Senior High School, Spartanburg, S.C. and received an A.A. degree from Spartanburg Junior College. He pursued his studies at Clemson University in S.C. until he entered the Air Force in January 1954 as an aviation cadet.

CADET:

January 1954 – June 1955

Lackland AFB, Texas
Columbus AFB, Mississippi   T-6
Greenville AFB, Mississippi

June 3, 1955

Marriage to his college
sweetheart   T-33
Ruth Searcy

GUNNERY

June 1955- August 1955
Laughlin AFB, Del Rio, Texas

Combat Training   F-86

August 1955- December 1955
Nellis AFB, Nevada

TACTICAL SQUADRONS SERVED

January 1956 – March 1960

George AFB, California
Tactical Fighter Squadrons:
436 & 476

F-104

October 27, 1959, son, Kevin Dale,
Was born to Ted and Ruth

March 1960 – March 1963

Wheelus AFB, Tripoli
Tactical Fighter Squadron 7272 Wing   F-100

April 1963 – August 1965.

Nellis AFB, Nevada
Command Post Controller
4520 Combat Crew Training Wing   F-105
Thunder Chief Combat Crew Training

September 1965 – June 1966

Kadena AFB, Okinawa
44th Tactical Fighter Squadron

June 1966 – September 1966   "THUD"

Korat AFB, Thailand
13th Fighter Squadron

KORAT AIR FORCE BASE

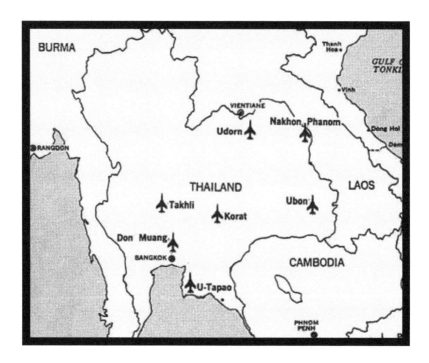

Korat was a front-line facility of the United States Air Force (USAF) during the Vietnam War from 1962 through 1975. The USAF forces at Korat were under the command of the United States Pacific Air Forces (PACAF). It was the primary headquarters (HQ) for the 388th Tactical Fighter Wing. Various parking areas and aprons alternately held both permanent and TDY/transient aircraft of all types. During the Vietnam War, the mission of the base was to conduct operations in support of U.S. commitments in Southeast Asia: North Vietnam, South Vietnam, Cambodia, and Laos.

During the Vietnam War, pilots from Korat RTAFB primarily flew interdiction, direct air support, armed reconnaissance, and fighter escort missions. The USAF mission at Korat began in April 1962, when one officer and fourteen airmen were temporarily assigned to the base as the joint U.S. Military Advisory Group (JUSMAG).

U.S. Army personnel were already stationed at Camp Friendship, a post adjacent south of the air base. In July 1964, approximately 500 persons were assigned to Korat to start the beginning of a tactical fighter operation. The construction of essential base facilities was initiated and completed by October 1964.

Ted – Korat
F105D

Tactical Fighter Squadron F-105D having MK-82 500-pound bombs being loaded prior to a mission at Korat in 1964

In December 1964, the 44th Tactical Fighter Squadron deployed to Korat from Kadena AB, Okinawa. The 44th would rotate pilots and personnel to Korat on a TDY (Temporary Duty) basis until 1966.

The 13th TFS was deployed to Korat RTAFB around 15 May 1966 and was mainly made up of pilots from the 44th Tactical Fighter Squadron out of Kadena AB. For some peculiar reason, the 44th TFS could not retain its numerical designator. Throughout the remainder of 1966 and until its deactivation in October 1967, the 13th participated in all major strikes to North Vietnam. Due to the high attrition rate, the Thailand-based Thunderchief squadrons were suffering. The 13th TFS was transferred to Udorn RTAFB as an F-4D Phantom II squadron on 20 October 1967; its aircraft and personnel were absorbed by the 44th TFS, which had earlier also absorbed men and machines from the 421st TFS at Korat.

The 44th TFS returned to Kadena AB, Okinawa, and assigned to the 18th TFW, but on 31 December 1966, it became only a paper organization without aircraft. The high loss rate of the F-105s in the two combat wings, at Korat and Takhli RTAFB, mandated the squadron to send its aircraft to Thailand as replacement aircraft. The 44th remained a "paper organization" until 23 April 1967, when it returned to Korat, absorbing the personnel, equipment, and resources of the 421st TFS.

September 26, 1966

4th Allied POW Wing:
Shot down on the 68th combat mission, September 26, 1966, thirty miles NNW of Hanoi by AAA. Unconscious during ejection. Awoke on the ground in the process of being captured.

Camps: Heartbreak Hotel; Zoo; Annex; Camp Faith; Hanoi Hilton; Dogpatch

Although not verified that this pilot was Ted Ballard, the plane type, month, and year coincided.

A PRAYER FOR COURAGE

When I was shot down and captured in the fall of 1966, the North Vietnamese had instigated a torture campaign to elicit certain information and propaganda from the prisoners. Besides trying to get me to write a war crimes confession, they really wanted to know the type of tactics we were using to deliver bombs. I knew that if I answered the questions it would mean the shoot-down and possible deaths of many American pilots, some of whom were my best friends. I refused to answer the questions and was tortured. I lost consciousness from the pain. When I awakened, the interrogation and torture resumed. During the next three days, I estimate that I went through between ten and fifteen torture sessions, during most of which I passed out from pain or shock or a combination of both. My left leg had been broken during bailout and my left hip was broken during one of the torture sessions. At times, when I awakened, I found myself untied, on the floor, and alone in the room. Soon the same men would return and the interrogation began again, with more questions concerning my military and civilian biography.

I gave more detail, but stuck generally to the same fabrications I had told earlier. During this period I was given no food, no water, and no medical attention. I continued to refuse to answer questions concerning military tactics. Sometime during the evening of the third day, I had again become unconscious from the torture. I looked up when I awakened and saw that the camp commander was the only one in the room. He looked at me and said, "Ballard, answer the question."

At this time, I was in bad shape and felt that I could not take any more torture. I was nervous, scared, confused, and in great pain. I said a silent prayer that went something like this: "Father,

please give me the courage to say 'no' to this man one more time."
I looked up at the commander and said "No." We continued
staring at each other for a few moments, and then he gathered his
papers and left the room. I was never again asked any questions
concerning military tactics. During the ensuing years I saw the
camp commander staring coldly at me a couple of times, but he
never spoke.

Over the months and years that followed, I realized that every
time I prayed for courage, I received courage. I no longer suffer
from torture or incarceration in a communist country, but the
need to make difficult decisions is with all of us, and the need to
pray for courage remains.

Ted Ballard

<u>Released March 4, 1973 – Operation Homecoming</u>

<u>March 1973 – August 1973</u>

 Hospitalized for medical evaluation of injuries incurred as a POW and for recovery   of war wounds.

<u>August 1973 – August 1974</u>

 War College, Maxwell AFB, Alabama
 (1974 Graduate)

<u>August 1974 – July 31, 1975</u>

 On Faculty of the War College

<u>1974 – 1975</u>

 Troy State University 1974 graduate, B.S. Degree
         1975 graduate, M.S. Degree

<u>August 1975</u>

 Retirement from USAF years
 22 years of service (January 1954 – August 1975)
 Rank: Lieutenant Colonel

<u>Memorable Experiences/Achievements</u>

• Military Awards & Recognitions

 Silver Star
 Legion of Merit
 Distinguished Flying Cross (2)

Bronze Star with V device (2)
Air Medal (8)
Purple Heart (2)

- Bachelor of Science and Master of Science Degrees from Troy State University

August 1975

Air Force Junior ROTC Instructor

After retirement from the Air Force, Lt. Col. Ballard joined the faculty of Gaffney Senior High School, Gaffney, S.C. as senior instructor in the Air Force Junior ROTC Program. Goal: to have the opportunity to guide hundreds of teenage students in today's environment.

May 1997

Retired from JROTC {second career} after 22 years.

CIVILIAN MEMORABLE EXPERIENCES/ACHIEVEMENTS

Civilian Awards and Recognitions:

- Gaffney Senior High School "Teacher of the Year"
- Cherokee County "Teacher of the Year"
- Three times selected by Gaffney High School's highest ranked students as "Outstanding Teacher"
- Paul Harris Fellow
- Honorary member of the 101st Airborne Division
- Warbird of the Year
- Deacon First Baptist Spartanburg

Numerous appearances as guest speaker at schools, churches, and civic organizations to acquaint the American people with the courage, devotion to duty, and teamwork displayed by the military while under extreme duress.

FAMILY DATA:

Wife: Ruth Searcy Ballard (20 September 1932 – 16 December 2015)
Retired from TimBar Corporation
Personnel and Accounting

Son: Kevin Dale Ballard (27 October 1959 – 4 May 2009)
M.D., PH.D. Director of Research and Development, National Medical Services (NMS Inc.), Pennsylvania

OPERATION HOMECOMING

RELEASE
March 4, 1973

Mrs. Ballard, Son Look Forward To Return Of Husband-Father

Hope, Relief And Joy Shared By POW Families

By AMY WEBB
Staff Writer

Hopeful that her husband will be returning home soon, after being a prisoner of war for six and a half years in North Vietnam, Mrs. Arthur T. Ballard Jr. of Lake Lure, is "relieved, overjoyed and hopeful that the recent peace settlements will be successful."

Mrs. Ballard lives at Lake Lure with her 13-year-old son, Kevin. She is librarian at Green Hill School. Kevin attends New Hope Elementary School in Rutherfordton. Her husband, Lt. Col. Ballard, was shot down over North Vietnam in 1966 while flying an AF 105 fighter plane from Thailand, where he was stationed.

At the time that her husband was shot down, he was a captain. Since that time he has been promoted to major and, a little over a year ago, he was made lieutenant colonel.

Mrs. Ballard first learned of her husband being listed as missing two and a half years ago. Her first letter was after he had been a prisoner for four years. Since that time letters have come sporadically. In 1971, she did not hear from her husband at all and that year was "really terrifying."

They are unable to write long letters as most would think, but must write on a form that is about five by seven inches in size. This form has seven printed lines on which to write. This is all the space that is allowed for writing.

"It is amazing how much you can say in so little space, but this involves writing and rewriting, trying to condense what you want to say in as few words as possible."

"I am able to send photographs with letters. They are stapled to the side. A package may be sent every two months. I have sent him vitamins, canned foods, freeze-dried foods and powdered milk."

Mrs. Ballard grew up in Lake Lure. Her husband originally is from Spartanburg, where his father, A. T. Ballard, still lives at 232 Greencreek Road. In the Air Force for 18 years, he was stationed in California, North Africa, Nevada and Okinawa before going to Thailand.

The Saturday before Mrs. Ballard received news that her husband was shot down, she had just received a princess ring, styled after the original princess ring of Thailand. This ring in Thailand is thought to bring good fortune and happiness to its wearer. The ring is set with emeralds.

She was informed of her husband's being officially listed as a prisoner by phone Jan. 27 and does not know when he will be coming home.

"Sixty days seem like a long time and the release of the prisoners is contingent upon the withdrawal of troops," she notes.

"I am more concerned about my husband's emotional damage than his physical condition."

Mrs. Ballard has been pleased with the response she has received from people throughout the states who expressed warmth and best wishes for her family's reunion.

"Thursday was Ted's 41st birthday and I had hoped that he would be on his way out."

From the Rutherfordton
Newspaper

"We never gave up hope."

The Following is from
The Forest City Courier, NC Newspaper

"Lt. Col. Ballard has served with honor
and for that, we honor him today."

Official Welcome Home ceremonies for Lt. Col Arthur T. Ballard of Lake Lure were held this weekend, and the people came from all parts of Rutherford County and surrounding areas to take part.

Almost a thousand braved the cold drizzle Saturday for a reception and ceremonies at Lake Lure, and thousands more (estimates ranged as high as ten thousand) thronged the streets of Rutherfordton Sunday afternoon for a parade in his honor.

For over an hour Saturday a continuous line filed through the Lake Lure Inn to meet Ballard, his wife, Ruth, and his son, Kevin. Outside, the Central, Chase, and East High bands played as the rain came down in a light mist. When the receiving line finally ended, everyone moved out to the Speakers' Platform in front of the Inn.

"This is the first time we have welcomed a prisoner of war home," said reception chairman Stover Dunagan, Jr., "but God willing, it will be the last."

Lake Lure Mayor Paul Wilson gave the official welcome: "I am proud to pay my respects to one who has given so many years of his life in the defense of his country," he said. "We are proud of you, and we are overjoyed to have you home at last."

A special guest for the ceremony was Pat Holshouser, wife of NC Governor James Holshouser. Her voice breaking several times with emotion, she said, "...there are no words to express the gratitude for having a prisoner of war home again. I cannot see or take part in one of these ceremonies without remembering my own father's homecoming." She said, "Gov. Holshouser would like to have been with you but was with the People's Day in Asheville. He would be especially proud to see so many people from North Carolina turn out to honor one of their returning prisoners of war."

Rep Robert A. Jonas of Forest City read a resolution honoring Lt. Col. Ballard, which had been adopted by the N.C. General Assembly two weeks ago, and Dunagan read telegrams from Lt. Gov. Jim Hunt, Rep. Roy A. Taylor, and Sen. Sam Ervin.

Rep. Richard Hines of Spartanburg said the S.C. General Assembly had adopted a similar resolution, and advised that "South Carolina is proud to join North Carolina to welcome home one we call a native son." Ballard is a native of Spartanburg.

Dunagan cited a speech given by Gen. Douglas MacArthur at West Point, and said, "Three words came up over and over again—duty and honor and country."

"There has probably never been a more professional soldier than MacArthur, and he strongly believed that the military leaders had to be the backbone of the leadership provided, and that by their doing their duty as they saw it, and by serving with honor and distinction, they brought honor to our nation.

"In the last few weeks we have heard the word honor used a great deal," said Dunagan. "As the POWs returned home and began speaking, they commented on their appreciation to their commander-in-chief, and to the people for allowing an honorable victory in the war, and for allowing them to return to their country with honor.

"In the last day or two, we learned (that) no one in Washington told them what to say. They decided on their own that those who came home first would not, in any way, jeopardize the safety of those who remained. I think this shows the real devotion that these men had to each other and that they will continue to have for all time.

"In many earlier wars—World War I and II—we had a definite

victory," said Dunagan. "When those wars ended and the military leaders came back, we had ticker tape parades, showered them with affection, and were elated over their glorious victory. In the last twenty years, we have had two conflicts in which there were no victories as such—only secession of hostilities. We did not have glorious leaders we could shower our affection on.

"Lt. Col. Ballard," said Dunagan, "is the last man who would want to have an occasion like this held for him. He recognizes that others in Vietnam are just as worthy of recognition. And the fact that he is here, in reasonably good health, is quite different from those who left a part of themselves in Vietnam, or perhaps never returned from Vietnam. But in a small way, we are recognizing all the men who served, were captured, or who died for this nation.

"Lt. Col. Ballard has served with honor and for that, we honor him today."

Lt. Col. Ballard was presented an engraved silver bowl as a "Welcome Home" gift from Rutherford County, and Tom McSwain presented the Ballards several other gifts "which show the great deal of love and respect the people of Rutherford County have for you."

Then Ballard took the stand: "Many times I dreamed of coming home, but I never anticipated the welcome to be anything like this.

"I thank you for this spectacular tribute to all those who served their country and especially to those who did not return. You all are wonderful, wonderful people and I love you all."

HOME TO SPARTANBURG

THEN TO MAXWELL AFB

By NANCY BROWER

Former POW's Wife Says Everyday Life Is 'Bliss'

by NANCY BROWER

During Ruth Ballard's six-year wait for her husband to be released from a prisoner of war camp in North Vietnam, she was interviewed by Times staffers on many occasions.

We came to greatly admire the pretty young wife for her courage and optimism as she waited at her mother's home near Lake Lure for the message that came this spring.

Air Force Lt. Col. Arthur 'T. (Ted) Ballard Jr., who was shot down over North Vietnam in September 1966, was reunited with his wife and their son, Kevin, 13, on March 7, 1973.

After the gala homecoming, 'the Ballards are settling into the routine of military life. Lt. Col. Ballard is attending air War College at Maxwell Air Force Base near Montgomery, Ala.

Ruth Ballard has written the following letter to the many Western North Carolinians who waited with her, and rejoiced at Colonel Ballard's release:

"Since the first flurry of press coverage that accompanied the returning prisoners of war from Southeast Asia ended, it seems that only the somber, unfortunate statistics have been newsworthy. There is a happy, beautiful side and I feel that this, also, should be told.

First of all, there is the indescribable bliss of being a family again, of watching a growing and strengthening father-son relationship, of witnessing the return of my husband's eagerness to once again lead a productive life. If this appears as wifely pride, surely in this instance it's justified.

The years of separation heightened our pleasure in furnishing a new home and returning to, the military.

The essence of our renewed joy is that we no longer take even the ordinary, routine aspects of life for granted. A leisurely stroll through the countryside at sunset, for instance, or sitting together in church on Sunday morning are privileges not taken lightly. Then the realization that we can start the day with Daddy at the head of the breakfast table, and when the work day is finished, the delightful sound of a car door closing and footsteps bounding up the, walk are daily sources of gratification.

Adjustments have been essential, of course, but they are trivial when compared with the compensation. Our philosophy is not to look backward with regret nor forward with fear; hence, it is not necessary 'to wait until evening to know how splendid the day has been.' "

Ruth Ballard

AIR FORCE
1954 –1975

USAF RETIREMENT
1975

AFJROTC INSTRUCTOR
1975 – 1997

Retirement
1997

Public Service

Speaker
at Public
Events

Often Assisted
by Ruth

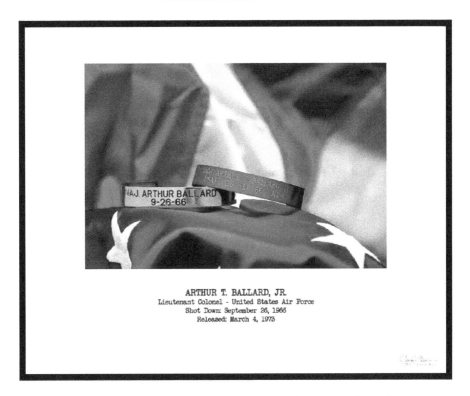

ARTHUR T. BALLARD, JR.
Lieutenant Colonel - United States Air Force
Shot Down: September 26, 1966
Released: March 4, 1973

This is perhaps the most important photograph I have ever made. When my father was serving in the Vietnam War in 1967, my mother obtained a POW bracelet, which bore the name of Arthur Ballard. Earlier this year, Mom and I found the bracelet in a box. Thanks to Google, I was able to find the now-retired Colonel Ballard and let him know we had the bracelet and wished to return it to him.

While Googling his name, I found a website that sells POW returnee bracelets that had a listing for Colonel Ballard. I got the returnee bracelet and then had the idea for this photo.

Now, some forty-three years later, Colonel Ballard has had his bracelet returned to him (one of many returned to him throughout the years), and my mom has his returnee bracelet in its place.

It's been an emotional experience for all of us. Corresponding with Col. Ballard has been an honor; he is an American hero and a very dear man. He was held captive for over six years of his life in North Vietnam.

Christopher Brocious

Clemson University[1]

Interview by Junior Will Hines

"Clemson University Research Project Preserves Veterans'
Stories for the Ages"
108th Training Command-Training Story by Sgt. Ken Scar

This interview was conducted for the Veterans History Project
(Library of Congress). Interviewee: Lt. Colonel Arthur Ballard of
the U.S. Air Force
Interviewer: William Robert Hines, Clemson University, Creative
Inquiry for Veterans History Project
Date: November 2nd, 2012

Date: 05.20.2015

Lt. Col. Ballard holds a POW/MIA bracelet that was worn in his
honor, while he was a captive in the infamous Hoa Lo prison, aka
the "Hanoi Hilton," and shows some of the mementos he kept
from his six-and-a-half-year stint as a prisoner of war.

---

[1]   http://virtual2.clemson.edu/veterans-history/index.php/vietnam-war
       And with the Library of Congress

Retired U.S. Air Force Col. Arthur T. Ballard was an F-105 fighter pilot during the Vietnam conflict, and had sixty-eight combat missions under his belt when he was shot down and captured Sept. 26, 1966. "I think it was small-arms fire, maybe thirty-two or fifty-seven-millimeter. The sky just filled up with that stuff," he recounted. "I don't remember a whole lot about the bailout. I woke up on the ground with a broken leg and a rifle stuck in my face." He was held as a prisoner of war for six and a half years in the infamous Hao Lo prison, aka the "Hanoi Hilton." Back in the United States, his wife Ruth didn't know if he was dead or alive, but she never gave up hope. Their harrowing, but ultimately inspiring, story is preserved forever in his fifty-eight-minute interview with Hines.

I was honored to be a part of the service at First Baptist Spartanburg honoring all veterans. I was also privileged to present, on behalf of Gov. Nikki Haley, a Letter and Certificate of Appreciation to Lt. Col. Ted Ballard for his service to country, state and community. Lt Col Ballard was shot down over Vietnam in 1966 and spent 6 1/2 years in a POW camp, where he was continuously tortured. He never lost his faith in God and prayer, which is what helped him survive this dark time in his life. He is a humble man who has never sought attention for himself, he only wanted to serve others. May God continue to bless him and all those who have served this country.

Representative Edward R. "Eddie" Tallon, Sr.
Republican – Spartanburg District 33 – Spartanburg County

The Family – Ruth, Kevin, Ted

Ruth and Kevin

Ruth and Ted at Home

Dr. Kevin D. Ballard*

NMS Labs

Kevin Ballard, M.D., Ph.D. – Director of Research & Development

Doctoral Level Scientist, responsible for Research and Development.

Company Description: National Medical Services is a full-service independent laboratory offering comprehensive analytical and consultative services in forensic and clinical toxicology, criminalistics, therapeutic drug monitoring, consumer product integrity testing, biopharmaceutical support services, environmental/occupational toxicology as well as research and development. Founded in 1970, NMS maintains a complete staff of forensic scientists and technical support personnel on call 24 hours a day all year round (24/7/365). The company's scientific results are supported through expert opinion reporting and expert testimony to stand up to the penetrating light of courtroom scrutiny.

Education:

   B.S. Degree, Wofford College, Spartanburg, S.C.
   M.D. Degree, College of Medicine, Medical University of South Carolina
   Ph.D. Degree in Molecular and Cellular Pharmacology and Experimental Therapeutics, Medical University of South Carolina

Board Memberships and Affiliations:

   American Society for Mass Spectrometry

Canadian Society for Mass Spectrometry
Provides peer review for the *Journal of the American Society for Mass Spectrometry*

*Dr. Ballard died prematurely on May 4, 2009. He was a nationally recognized expert on forensic science and provided courtroom testimony in many high-profile cases, such as:

New York vs. Michael Swango,
California vs. Orenthal James Simpson,
New Jersey vs. Josh Pompey,
Connecticut vs. Alex Kelley and many others.

"THUD"

In 1951 Republic Aviation began a project to develop a supersonic tactical fighter-bomber to replace the F-84F. The result was the F-105 Thunderchief, later affectionately nicknamed the "Thud." The prototype YF-105A first flew in October 1955, but the first F-105D did not fly until June 1959. A total of 833 Thunderchiefs of all types were built, including 610 F-105Ds.

The U.S. Air Force sent F-105s to Southeast Asia shortly after the Tonkin Gulf incident in the summer of 1964. The USAF operated the F-105D extensively in the air campaign against North Vietnam called Rolling Thunder. Although designed as a nuclear strike aircraft, the F-105 could carry a total of over 12,000 pounds of conventional ordnance—a heavier bomb load than a World War II B-17. The F-105 was gradually replaced by the F-4 Phantom, and the USAF withdrew the last F-105D from service in July 1980.

The aircraft on display is painted and marked as it appeared while serving in the 357th Tactical Fighter Squadron, 355th Tactical Fighter Wing, based at Takhli Royal Thai Air Base in Thailand. The nickname

Memphis Belle II refers to the B-17F that carried the same artwork during WWII. The two red stars under the cockpit represent the two MiG kills it claimed during the Southeast Asia War. It arrived at the museum in April 1990.

TECHNICAL NOTES:
Armament: One M61 Vulcan 20mm cannon and more than 12,000 lbs. of ordnance
Engine: One Pratt & Whitney J75-P-19W of 24,500 lbs. thrust
Maximum speed: 1,390 mph
Cruising speed: 778 mph
Range: 2,206 miles
Ceiling: 51,000 ft.
Span: 34 ft. 11 in.
Length: 64 ft. 5 in.
Height: 19 ft. 8 in.
Weight: 52,838 lbs. maximum

Acknowledgements:

* Christopher Brocious of Brocious Photography:
  http://chrisbrocious.com/
  (His extraordinary generosity to the family is appreciated)

* "Clemson University Research Project Preserves Veterans' Stories for the Ages"
  108th Training Command-Training Story by Sgt. Ken Scar
  http://virtual2.clemson.edu/veterans-history/index.php/vietnam-war

* The Air Force Historical Studies Division:
  http://www.airforcemag.com/archives/1999

* The Asheville (N.C.) Times

* The Forest City (N,C,) Courier

* The Rutherford County (N.C.) News

* The Spartanburg (S.C.) Herald Journal

* The Times News (Hendersonville, N.C.)

* This Week (Rutherford County, N.C.)

* http://www.bing.com/images/vietnam

Editor's Note:

It has been a privilege to compile, edit, and design this book for the family of Lt. Col. Ballard. His personal sacrifices in his service to our country, the public service he has freely given to our home state of South Carolina, his extraordinary example of strong personal integrity, Christian ethics, and his love of family and country will forever stand as an example for our children.

Carrie's Creek (Family Historian)

As Orpheus sings

Thus does my heart hear the Muse
When forever the great say naught

What will the future partake
When will our people forsake

The doomed naysayer who looks
but cannot see

That, directed by Love not Hate
These warriors will shape

The swords into plowshares
For the land they clear of fear

Then as Orpheus sings
The Stones and Trees will Dance

PART FOUR: TIMELINE

Lt. Col. Arthur T. Ballard, USAF (Ret.)

From the Dungeons of North Vietnam – Return With Honor is a memoir of one USAF jet pilot's shoot-down over North Vietnam and his capture in September 1966, while on a military combat mission. This memoir, of significant historical value, vividly recounts the details of Lt. Colonel Ballard's capture, the torture, and the living conditions that he and his fellow POWs endured during their years as prisoners of war in the prison camps of North Vietnam, until their release in 1973.

Upon his retirement from the United States Force in 1975, Lt. Colonel Ballard accepted the position as senior instructor of the Air Force Junior Reserve Officer Training Corps at Gaffney Senior High School, in Gaffney, S.C. He retired from the AFJROTC Program in 1997 and now pursues his interest in the educational needs of young people through his established endowments with Wofford College and Spartanburg Methodist College, in his hometown of Spartanburg, South Carolina.

CPSIA information can be obtained
at www.ICGtesting.com
Printed in the USA
LVHW01*1524180118
562591LV00002B/2/P